1000 THINGS
WORTH KNOWING

1000 THINGS WORTH KNOWING

"That all who read may know"

NATHANIEL C. FOWLER, JR.

COSIMO CLASSICS

NEW YORK

PREFACE

This book contains more than one thousand facts, many of which are not generally known to the average person; but all of them are of interest to humankind, and a knowledge of many of them is essential.

The author has used the simplest English, and has avoided, as far as posible, all technical or scientific terms. He has endeavored not to fall into the common error of making his explanations harder to understand than the subjects treated.

This book is not intended for the scientist, nor does it claim to be exhaustive.

In the space of a few hundred pages the writer has presented the thousand or more things which are really worth knowing, and which are usually described at unprofitable length and without that simplicity of expression so essential to clearness.

To find what you
want consult the
Index.

Abbreviations in Common Use

Abbreviations given are those which are frequently used. For complete list of abbreviations, the reader is referred to any unabridged dictionary.

A. B. or B. A.—Bachelor of Arts.

A. D.—In the Year of Our Lord.

Agt.—agent.

A. M. or M. A.—Master of Arts.

bbl.—barrel.

B. Agr.—Bachelor of Agriculture.

B. C.—Before Christ.

B. D.—Bachelor of Divinity.

B. L.—Bachelor of Laws.

B. M. or B. Mus.—Bachelor of Music.

B. Pd.—Bachelor of Pedagogy.

B. Ph.—Bachelor of Philosophy.

B. S.—Bachelor of Surgery.

B. S. or B. Sc.—Bachelor of Science.

Capt.—Captain.

C. E.—Civil Engineer.

C. O. D.—Cash (collect) on Delivery.

Col.—Colonel.

D. C.—District of Columbia, District Court.

D. C. L.—Doctor of Canon Law.

D. D. S. or D. M. D.—Doctor of Dental Surgery.

D.D.—Doctor of Divinity.

D. Litt.—Doctor of Literature.

D. M. or D. Mus.—Doctor of Music.

D. Ph.—Doctor of Philosophy.

Dr.—Doctor.

D. Sc.—Doctor of Science.

D. V. S.—Doctor of Veterinary Surgery.

E.D.—Doctor of Electricity.

E. E.—Electrical Engineer

F. O. B.—Free on board.

G. A. R.—Grand Army of the Republic.

Gen. or Gen'l—General.

Gov.—Governor.

Hon.—Honorable.

i. e.—that is.

int.—interest.

J. C. D.—Doctor of Civil Law.

J. D.—Doctor of Laws.

J. P.—Justice of the Peace.

Jr. or Jun.—Junior.

lat.—latitude.

lb.—pound.

Lieut. or Lt.—Lieutenant.

Litt. B. or Lit. B.—Bachelor of Literature.

Litt. D. or Lit. D.—Doctor of Literature.

LL. B.—Bachelor of Laws.

LL. D.—Doctor of Laws.

M. Agr.—Master of Agriculture.

Maj.—Major.

M. C.—Member of Congress.

M. D.—Doctor of Medicine.

M. P.—Member of Parliament.

M. P. C.—Member of Parliament in Canada.

M. S.—Master of Science.

ms.—manuscript.

Mus. B. — Bachelor of Music.

Mus. D.—Doctor of Music.

Pd. B.—Bachelor of Pedagogy.

Pd. D.—Doctor of Pedagogy.

Ph. B.—Bachelor of Philosophy.

Ph. D.—Doctor of Philosophy.

P. M.—Postmaster.

P. O.—Post Office.

Prof.—Professor.

P. S.—Postscript.

Rev.—Reverend.

S. B. or Sc. B.—Bachelor of Science.

Sc. D.—Doctor of Science.

S. T. B.—Bachelor of Sacred Theology.

S. T. D.—Doctor of Sacred Theology.

Rt. Hon.—Right Honorable.

Rt. Rev.—Right Reverend.

V. Rev.—Very Reverend.

yd.—yard.

yr.—year.

Acetylene Gas.—Acetylene gas is used largely for the search-lamps on automobiles. It is composed of carbon and hydrogen.

Adventists.—A religious sect whose members believe that the second coming of Christ is near at hand. There are over 114,000 communicants and ministers.

Æolian Harp.—This instrument was invented in the 17th century and was named after Æolus, the god of the winds. It is of the simplest construction, and its music is produced by the vibration of the strings automatically moved by the winds. In construction it is a rectangular box of thin boards of a few inches in depth and width and of sufficient length to extend across a window so that the breeze may pass through it. The strings are stretched lengthwise across the top of the box, and may be tuned by increasing or decreasing their tension.

Age.—About 50 per cent. of the persons living in the United States are under 20 years of age, 45 per cent. from 20 to 60 years, and 5 per cent. over 60 years, the average age being about 25 years. This average seems low, and is due largely to infant mortality. If the percentage was taken excluding those under 15 years of age it would be very much higher.

Agricultural Implement Industry.—Capital invested, about $260,000,000, and an annual output of about $150,000,000. About 60,000 people are employed.

Alaska.—Alaska is the only territory of the United States, the Hawaiian Islands, Porto Rico, and the Philippines being known as Possessions. It has an area of over 590,000 square miles, and a population of about 65,000. Its climate is semipolar.

Algebra.—The discoverer or the first user of algebra is unknown. It is said that Diophantus wrote it in 170 A. D., and he may have been its inventor. It was brought into Spain in about 900. Its signs are said to have been used first in 1544, but algebra did not come into common use until 1590. Descartes applied algebra to geometry in 1637.

Almanacs.—The word "almanac" is of Saxon origin, and probably the first almanac was published in 1470, and the first in English in 1673.

Amazons.—An ancient body of warlike women, ruled by a queen, who allowed no man to live with them. They were opposed to marriage and resolved to form a female state. They burned off their right breasts that they might better use the bow and javelin. This custom is the origin of the name "Amazons" or "breastless ones."

Apostles' Creed.—Considered by most Biblical students as the earliest form of Christian creed. It is attributed directly to the Apostles. It is doubtless the formula of belief that existed in all the early Latin churches. It was made a part of public worship of the Christian church at Antioch, and introduced into the Roman Catholic Church in the eleventh century, and subsequently into the Church of England.

April Fool's Day.—Its origin is unknown,

but it is supposed to follow an ancient pageant custom of playing tricks on the first day of April.

Arbor Day.—A day of varying date officially set apart in the United States and Canada for the planting of trees, shrubs, etc. It was the intention to have this day observed chiefly by the children of the public schools. Its observance has resulted in the planting of millions of trees.

Arithmetic.—While the inventor or discoverer of arithmetic is unknown, it is said that it was brought from Egypt into Greece in 600 B. C. Euclid is the author of the oldest treatise upon arithmetic and wrote it about 300 B. C. The arithmetic of decimals began in 1482, and the first arithmetic in English was printed in 1522.

Artesian Wells.—An artesian well is one made by boring perpendicularly into the earth. The oldest known well of this kind was sunk in Europe in 1126. Probably the most famous one is near Paris, which was bored in 1833, bringing water from a depth of 1792 feet. From this well 516 gallons of water flow per minute. In Missouri there is one well 2197 feet deep, and another nearly 4000 feet deep. The invention of the artesian well is undoubtedly due to the Chinese.

Artificial Ice.—The artificial manufacture of ice is of somewhat recent origin, and there are over 2,000 ice-making plants in the United States, exclusive of those used by packing houses and others for the making of their own ice. Artificial ice-making showed an increase of 81 per cent. during the last few years.

Atlantic Cable.—The original or, rather, the first permanent cable, was laid in July, 1866, connecting Ireland with Newfoundland; but an earlier cable was laid between the foregoing points, which was lost in construction. This lost cable, however, was recovered and completed.

In 1868 a cable was laid from France to Duxbury, Mass. In 1873 the fourth Atlantic cable connected Ireland and Trinity Bay, New Foundland. Several cables have been subsequently laid, and are maintained.

Considerable difficulty was experienced in obtaining the right kind, and a sufficient current, of electricity, which would carry the message several thousand miles under water, and not pass from the cable into the water itself.

Two keys are used, which, when depressed, transmit respectively positive and negative currents coming from the connected batteries. The current does not pass directly into the cable, but enters what is known as a condenser, and from there reaches the wire itself. This increases the force of the current and overcomes interfering earth currents.

Originally the messages were received by a reflecting galvanometer. Upon the magnet of this instrument was placed a small curved mirror, and in front of it was a lighted lamp behind a frame with a vertical slit. The light from the lamp passed through the slit and fell upon the surface of the mirror. The flashes of light moving with the movements of the suspended needle, indicated the message sent. Because of the delicacy of the instrumnt, it was difficult to translate the telegraphic code. The system has been entirely superseded by the use of the syphon galvanometer. This needle is affected by the currents, and moves in response to the opening and closing of the telegraphic key. It consists of a small hollow needle, which swings between two fixed magnets. A very soluble analine ink is allowed to flow through the tube. The mouth of this tube is suspended a very small fraction above a strip or roll of white paper, which moves automatically. The vibration or movements of the needle allow the ink to flow in irregular lines or curves upon the moving paper. These irregularities or curves indicate letters, which are easily read by the receiving operator.

Cable dispatches now are recorded, when formerly they had to be read as they were seen, with the impossibility of retaining an automatic record of them.

Professor Morse, the inventor of telegraphy, may be considered the inventor of the cable, although he had little to do with its mechanical construction. To Mr. Cyrus W. Field must be given much of the credit, for its accomplishment was largely due to his foresight and energy.

The cable consists of several copper wires imbedded in gutta percha or similar substance, which is one of the best nonconductors of electricity. The cable, with its several wires and coverings or insulation, has a circumference equal to that of the old-fashioned three-cent piece. Several wires are imbedded into the insulation, so as to insure better connection.

The cable is laid by steamers built for the purpose. They travel over a charted route, and, unscientifically speaking, throw the cable overboard. Of course, no cable could be constructed of a length that would reach across the ocean. New pieces are, therefore, spliced in as conditions require. If the sea is too rough for the laying of the cable, the end is buoyed and picked up when the weather changes. The cable lies upon the bottom of the ocean, and, as the bottom of the ocean is as irregular as the surface of the earth, with its mountains, plateaus, and valleys, there is always danger of the cable being broken or injured, although there is, of course, absolute quiet at the bottom of the ocean. Then, many feet, or even a mile, of cable may be stretched between two projecting points, and the strain may part it in time.

The process of locating a break or injury is very interesting. The cable fails to work. The operator stationed at either end discharges electricity into the cable, and, although it does not reach the other side, he can, by a delicate instrument, locate approximately the place of parting or where injury has occurred. The repair steamer sails for the place. With grappling irons it brings the cable to the surface; but as the location of the break cannot be determined accurately, the electrician on board must determine which way to sail to locate the place of the trouble. He attaches the cable to a battery on board, and opens connection with the land. If the break, for example, is between him and Europe, the European operator will not respond, but he will receive a reply from the American operator. He then directs the vessel's course towards Europe. The cable, when it is taken on board, is run on pulley wheels, one in the bow and one in the stern of the vessel, and the vessel sails slowly under the cable. As the vessel is two or three hundred feet long, several hundred feet of cable will be exposed. The cable is watched carefully, and the break or injury will be easily located. When it is, the operator connects the cable with the batteries, and then telegraphs in the direction opposite to that from which he received a reply. If his message goes through, the receiving operator will respond. If a reply comes, he knows he has located the break; if no reply is received, there must be other breaks in the same direction. The break is repaired, and the steamer sails on until it finds another break or injury. I have attempted to explain this in the simplest words. It is obvious that a scientific explanation would be unintelligible to the average reader.

Atmosphere.—While accurate figures are impossible, and while astronomers somewhat differ, it is generally conceded that the earth's atmosphere extends from the surface to an altitude of about 40 miles. It is theoretically or scientifically accepted that the density of the atmosphere at only a few miles from the surface of the earth is not sufficient to support life.

Aurora Borealis.—Until electricity was discovered, the origin of the aurora borealis was unknown, and was supposed to be of supernatural origin. Even to-day its exact composition or source is more or less of a mystery, but it is generally supposed that it is caused by the recomposition of positive and negative electricity. It exists only in the regions of the poles, although its light is seen to a moderate degree over the greater part of the earth.

Automobiles.—All vehicles used on the common highway, and propelled by any mechanical power, whether it be by steam, gasoline, or electricity, are known as automobiles or motor cars. The invention of the automobile is very recent, although steam-propelled carriages were in existence more than 50 years ago. Over eight million are in daily use in the United States, and have an estimated value of about ten billion dollars.

Bank of England.—Established in the city of London in 1694. Although a private institution, it is under Government control, and constitutes the Treasury of the Empire, England having no national treasury like that of the United States. It is managed by a governor, deputy-governor, and twenty-four directors.

Bastile.—The name given to a French prison, built between 1370 and 1383, originally as a fortress, but later used as a regular prison. It was destroyed by a mob in 1789. It was the seat of the terrible cruelties practiced in the early days.

Bayreuth Festival.—A musical festival held at the National Theatre in Bayreuth, Bavaria, which was built for the performance of the works of Wagner. The foundation stone of the building was laid in 1872, and Wagner himself opened the theatre in 1876 with a grand production of the " Nibelungen Trilogy."

Bible.—Between the eighth and tenth centuries parts of the Bible were translated into Anglo-Saxon, and in 1290 appeared an English version of the Psalms. In 1380 the New Testament was finished, and a little later the Old Testament was fully translated. The so-called King James Bible was published in 1610, and remained in common use until the present revisions were made.

Bible Statistics

	Old Testament	New Testament	Total
Books	39	27	66
Chapters	929	260	1,189
Verses	33,214	7,959	41,173
Words	593,493	181,253	774,746
Letters	2,728,100	838,380	3,566,480

The shortest chapter is Psalm cxvii; Ezra vii, 21, contains all the letters of the alphabet except j; Esther viii, 9, is the longest verse; John xi, 35, is the shortest verse. There is no word of more than six syllables in the Bible.

Bi-Metallism.—A monetary system in which gold and silver are put on the same plane as regards mintage and legal-tender.

Birth Stones.—January, garnet; February, amethyst; March, bloodstone or jasper; April, diamond or sapphire; May, emerald or carnelian; June, agate or chalcedony; July, ruby or onyx; August, sardonyx; September, chrysolite; October, opal or beryl; November, topaz; December, turquoise.

Blind.—In the United States there are about 57,000 blind persons, a little more than half of whom are totally blind. Of this number about 32,000 are males, and about 25,000 females.

Blood-heat.—The normal temperature of man is about 98½° Farenheit. This temperature is maintained with a variation of not more than two degrees, whether one lives on the Equator or in the Arctic regions. Any great deviation is likely to prove fatal. Animals have about the same temperature as man, while the blood of birds is from eight to ten degrees warmer. Reptiles, fishes, and all invertebrates maintain temperatures about the same as that of their environmnt.

Blue-Grass Region.—An undulating plateau in the north-central part of Kentucky, covering about 10,000 square miles, is known as the Blue-Grass Region. The underlying rock for 150 or more feet is blue limestone, very rich in phosphate of lime. This rock crumbles on exposure to the air and enriches the soil. Tobacco and hemp have two crops a year and grow to a great height. Meadow grass grows continuously. The Blue-Grass Region for many years has been the centre of the blooded stock of America.

Boxers.—A Chinese secret society supposed to be semireligious and semipatriotic. The Boxers originally believed that they were immune from death or physical injury, and that they could, with safety, attack any foreign foe.

Brain.—As the action of the brain has not, as yet, been seen by man, no one, at the present day, knows just what it is, beyond its merely physiological or mechanical substance. It is said that the brain of the normal man contains over 300,000,000 cells, and that about 3,000 are destroyed every minute. If this is the case, then a new brain appears once in 60 days. The normal brain has a volume of from 58 to 105 cubic inches. The brain of the Anglo-Saxon and German, and of other civilized nations, averages the larger number, while the negro brain occupies a space of about 96 cubic inches, and some Australian natives have brains of only about 58 cubic inches. The male brain is about ten per cent. heavier or larger than that of the female. The most intelligent animals have only about 16 ounces of brains. The size of the brain, if it is not below normal, does not appear to influence the intellectuality of its possessor. Men with small brains may have larger mind capacity than some of those possessing brains weighing several ounces more. It would appear, then, that the size of the brain, unless it be unusually small, has little to do with its quality.

Bread.—It is said that the Chinese were the first bread makers, and that they made bread from wheat and rice as early as 1998 B. C. Probably the first bread made from yeast was baked in England in about 1634. Aërated bread, which rises from carbolic acid gas injected into the dough, became somewhat common in 1857, but practically all bread, bakery-made or home-made, owes its leavening to yeast or baking powder.

Breakfast Foods.—Breakfast foods in the main are composed of either corn, wheat, or oat products, a few being made of barley, starch, and tapioca. They are sold under trade names, and most of them need no cooking by the consumer, as they were properly cooked at the mill. Usually they are made of only one grain, and to some of them is added a small quantity of salt. Most of them are pure products and are unadulterated, but few, if any of them, are any better than the grain sold in bulk, which can be purchased for about 4 cents per pound.

Brook Farm.—A famous socialistic community, originated by George Ripley and others in 1841 and located near West Roxbury, Massachusetts. The estate consisted of two hundred acres, and a company of edu-

cated men and women settled here to work
out an experiment, in which each person performed a certain share of necessary manual
labor.   The enterprise was abandoned as an
utter failure in 1846. Among the persons connected with the movement were George Ripley, Charles A. Dana, Ralph Waldo Emerson,
Nathaniel Hawthorne, George William Curtis,
Theodore Parker, Margaret Fuller, and Dr.
Channing.

Calculating Interest

To find the interest on any sum, at any rate
per cent., and for any length of time: 1st.
Multiply the principal by the rate per cent.,
expressed in hundredths; this will give the
interest for one year.   2nd. Find the number
of days remaining by consulting the calendar;
and multiply the principal by as many hundredths as there are days, and for 3 per cent.,
divide the product by 120; for 4 per cent.,
divide by 90; for 5 per cent., divide by 72; for
6 per cent., divide by 60; for 7 per cent., divide
by 52; for 8 per cent., divide by 45; for 9 per
cent., divide by 40; for 10 per cent., divide by
36; and for 12 per cent., divide by 30.   This
will give the interest for the days.   3rd. Add
the two items of interest, and the sum will
be the entire interest.

To find the number of days from any day
of any one month to the same day of any
other month.

From	Jan.	Feb.	Mar.	Apr.	May	June	July	Aug.	Sept	Oct.	Nov.	Dec.
To January ...	365	334	306	275	245	214	184	153	122	92	61	31
February	31	365	337	306	276	245	215	184	153	123	92	62
March	59	28	365	334	304	273	243	212	181	151	120	90
April	90	59	31	365	335	304	274	243	212	182	151	121
May	120	89	61	30	365	334	304	273	242	212	181	151
June	151	120	92	61	31	365	335	304	273	243	212	182
July	181	150	122	91	61	30	365	334	303	273	242	212
August	212	181	153	122	92	61	31	365	334	304	273	243
September	243	212	184	153	123	92	62	31	365	335	304	274
October	273	242	214	183	153	122	92	61	30	365	334	304
November	304	273	245	214	184	153	123	92	61	31	365	335
December	334	303	275	244	214	183	153	122	91	61	30	365

N. B.—In leap year. if the last day of February comes between, add one day to the number in the table.

Canals.—The Suez Canal is 103 miles long with a depth of 35 feet, and is 108 feet wide at the bottom. It cost $127,000,000. The Manchester Canal, between Manchester and Liverpool, is 35½ miles long, with a depth of 28 feet, and 120 feet wide at the bottom. It cost $85,000,000. The canal connecting the Baltic and North Seas is 61 miles long, 36 feet deep, and has a bottom width of 72 feet. It cost $40,000,000. The Panama Canal, opened for navigation Aug. 15, 1914, is about 50 miles in length, with a width of 300 feet, and a minimum depth of 41 feet. The United States Government paid $50,000,000 to the new French Canal Company and the Republic of Panama, for property rights and franchises, and the total cost, exclusive of fortifications, was $375,000,000. The Canal Zone extends for 5 miles on either side of the canal. The United States pays annually $250,000 to the Panama Republic for this strip of land. Total receipts to July 1, 1920 were $33,350,048; total costs of operating and maintaining were $36,771,473.

Capacity of Cisterns or Wells.—For each ten inches in depth, a cistern 2 feet in diameter will hold 19 gallons; 2½ ft., 30 g.; 3 ft., 44 g.; 3½ ft., 60 g.; 4 ft., 78 g.; 4½ ft., 97 g.; 5 ft., 122 g.; 5½ ft., 148 g.; 6 ft., 176 g.; 6½ ft., 207 g.; 7 ft., 240 g.; 7½ ft., 275 g.; 8 ft., 313 g.; 8½ ft., 353 g.; 9 ft., 396 g.; 9½ ft., 461 g.; 10 ft., 489 g.; 11 ft., 592 g.; 12 ft., 705 g.; 13 ft., 827 g.; 14 ft., 959 g.; 15 ft.; 1101 g.; 20 ft., 1958 g.; 25 ft., 3059 g.

Capitol at Washington.—The Capitol is situated in latitude 38° 53′ 20″.4 north and longitude 77° 00′ 35″.7 west from Greenwich. It fronts east, and stands on a plateau eighty-eight feet above the level of the Potomac. The entire length of the building from north to south is 751 feet 4 inches, and its greatest dimension from east to west 350 feet. The area covered by the building is 153,112 square feet. The dome of the original central building was constructed of wood, covered with copper. This was replaced in 1856 by the present structure of cast iron. The entire weight of iron used is 8,909,200 pounds. The dome is crowned by a bronze statue of Freedom, which is nineteen feet, six inches, high and weighs 14,985 pounds. The height of the dome above the base line of the east front is 287 feet 5 inches. The height from the top of the balustrade of the building is 217 feet 11 inches. The greatest diameter at the base is 135 feet 5 inches. The rotunda is 97 feet 6 inches in diameter, and its height from the floor to the top of the canopy is 180 feet 3 inches. The Senate Chamber is 113 feet 3 inches in length, 80 feet 3 inches in width, and 36 feet in height. The galleries will accommodate 1,000 persons. The Representatives' Hall is 139 feet in length, by 93 feet in width, and 36 feet in height. The room now occupied by the Supreme Court was, until 1859, the Senate Chamber. Previous to that time the court occupied the room immediately beneath, now used as a law library.

Celluloid.—Celluloid, from which many toilet articles and imitations of ivory are made, is composed from the cellulose found in cotton cloth or raw cotton. It is treated with a solution of nitric acid which forms it into a pulp very much like paper pulp. It is then washed with water, which removes most of the acid. It is partially hardened and camphor gum mixed with it, when it is rolled into sheets and thoroughly dried. In order to manipulate it, it is softened by steam and then hardened by drying. Celluloid is very inflammable. Wearers of celluloid combs and other ornaments should not expose themselves to fire.

Certified Checks.—A personal check becomes certified when across it is written " certified," with the name of the bank and the signature of the cashier or other official. The bank, then, becomes liable for the amount of the check. If the maker of a check has his check certified, he is jointly responsible with the bank for its payment, but if the receiver of the check has it certified, the maker of the check is released from all responsibility.

Chemical Composition of Man

Huxley's table on the chemical composition of man of the average weight of 154 pounds was for years the standard, but it has recently been superseded by a new one compiled by the French Academy of Sciences. The table is appended:

Elements	Pounds	Ounces	Grains
Oxygen	111	8	0
Hydrogen	21	6	0
Carbon	21	0	0
Nitrogen	3	10	0
Phosphorus	1	2	88
Calcium	2	0	0
Sulphur	0	0	219
Chlorine	0	2	47
Sodium (salt)	0	2	116
Iron	0	0	100
Potassium	0	0	290
Magnesium	0	0	12
Silica	0	0	2

—*World Almanac.*

Chess.—Chess is one of the oldest, and probably the most scientific, game known. Its origin is mysterious. It was mentioned in

Oriental literature about 2000 B. C. It was originally played in India, Persia, and Arabia, and subsequently was known in Spain and Western Europe. It is said that it was invented in order to teach the art of war.

Christmas.—A festival commemorating the birth of Christ. Said to have been observed as early as 98. Some of the early Christians celebrated the event in May; others in April and in June. In the fifth century, it was generally observed on the 25th of December.

Circulation of the Blood.—Although even the savage had seen and spilled blood, the circulation of the blood, and the part that it plays in the human machine, was not discovered until about 1616, by the English physiologist, William Harvey.

Climate and Temperature.—Climatic conditions are dependent upon heat, moisture, and altitude. The greatest heat is at the equator and diminishes as one aproaches either pole, but a place of high altitude near the equator may be cooler than another farther removed from it and occupying a shut-in or low position. It is warm at times, even near the poles. The climate is also affected by the winds, and very greatly by the ocean, and especially by ocean currents. Take England, for example: it is considerably further north than Boston or New York City, and yet its climate is much warmer or milder, due to its proxmity to the

Gulf Stream. Land near the ocean is likely to be cooler in summer on account of its prevailing winds, and warmer in winter because a large body of water reduces the cold. It is well-known that towns on the seashore do not suffer from extreme cold as much as do those in the same latitude further inland. The altitude has much to do with climate. Even in the warmest countries, where the heat is intense, the tops of high mountains are clothed with snow. Forests, by their shade, reduce the temperature.

Coal Industry.—In the United States the coal fields have an area of exceeding 160,000 square miles, but it is supposed that there are at least 310,000 square miles which contain coal. The estimated quantity of the available coal is exceeding 3,000,000,000,000 tons.

Cocoa Industry.—The world produces about 730,000,000 pounds of cocoa annually. The English Colonies about 320,000,000, Brazil about 121,000,000, Ecuador about 88,000,-000, San Tomaso about 67,000,000, San Domingo about 55,000,000, Venezuela about 41,-000,000.

Coffee Industry.—Brazil, about 1,300,000,-000, Central America, about 201,000,000, Venezuela, about 97,000,000, other South American countries about 78,000,000, Hayti and Santo Domingo, about 84,000,000, Mexico, about 43,-000,000, Porto Rico, about 34,000,000, Jamaica, about 10,000,000; a total of nearly 2,000,000,-

000 pounds annually. The United States consumes about 1,210,000,000 pounds a year.

Coin.—Money, in the form of metallic coins, probably superseded all other legal tenders. The first record of the coining of silver was in 869 B. C., and it was made in Rome as early as 269 B. C., and in Great Britain 25 years before the Christian Era. Gold was first coined in England in 1087. Copper money was introduced by James I of England in 1620. The United States mint began to coin money in 1793.

Colosseum.—The building of the Colosseum at Rome began in A. D. 80. It covers about five acres of ground, and has a seating capacity for nearly 90,000 persons. It was built in the form of an oval, with a diameter varying from 312 to 515 feet, the height being from 160 to 180 feet. In its arena, the gladiators fought among themselves and with wild beasts. At its dedication by Titus, 5,000 wild beasts were killed, and the celebration lasted for nearly a hundred days. Occasionally the arena was flooded with water, and sea fights took place.

Comets.—Comets are supposed to be made up of an innumerable number of meteors, with millions of miles of burning gas. They have regular orbits, but they have not been fully established and are more or less eccentric. They are not supposed to shine by their own

light, but to obtain it by reflection.   The orbit
of comets was discovered by Hadley in 1682,
who predicted their return.   Sometimes the
head and tail part, and remain so.   Their number is unknown, but there are supposed to be
thousands of them.   The comet formerly was
looked upon as a source of danger, and it was
supposed that the near approach of one of
them would destroy the earth or any other
celestial body.   Recent research, however, indicates that comets have not sufficient density
to cause damage, although they might affect
the atmosphere.   The principal thing to be
feared, however, if there is any danger, is that
the envelopment of the earth by the comet's
gas would destroy life, but most astronomers
have agreed that the atmosphere of the earth
would be sufficient protection.   So far as is
known, no comet has ever caused any injury,
and as they have existed from time immemo-
rial, there would appear to be no reason for
alarm.

Common Measurements

Diameter of a circle × 3.1416 = Circumference.

Radius of a circle × 6.283185 = Circumference.

Square of the radius of a circle × 3.1416 =
Area.

Square of the diameter of a circle × .7854 =
Area.

Square of the circumference of a circle ×
.07958 = Area.

Half the circumference of a circle × half its
diameter = Area.

Circumference of a circle × .159155 = Radius.

Square root of the area of a circle × .56419
= Radius.

Circumference of a circle × 31831 = Diameter.

Square root of the area of a circle × 1.12839
= Diameter.

Diameter of a circle × .86 = Side of inscribed equilateral triangle.

Diameter of a circle × .7071 = Side of an
inscribed square.

Circumference of a circle × .226 = Side of
an inscribed square.

Circumference of a circle × .282 = Side of
square of equal area.

Diameter of a circle × .8862 = Side of a
square of equal area.

Base of a triangle × one-half the altitude =
Area.

The product of both diameters × .7854 =
Area of an ellipse.

Surface of a sphere × one-sixth of its diameter = Solidity.

Circumference of a sphere × its diameter =
Surface.

Square of the circumference of a sphere ×
.3183 = Surface.

Square root of the surface of a sphere $\times$ 1.772454 = Circumference.

Square of one of its sides $\times$ 6 = Surface of a cube.

Area of the base of a square, round or triangular pyramid, or of a cone, $\times$ one-third of its altitude = Solidity.

Area of square $\times$ .7854 = Area of largest circle within it.

Area of circle $\times$ .625 = Area of largest square within it.

Spheres.—Square of circumference $\times$ .3183 = Surface of sphere.

Square of diameter $\times$ 3.1416 = Surface of sphere.

Square root of surface $\times$ .5642 = Diameter of sphere.

Cube of diameter $\times$ .5236 = Solidity of sphere.

Cube of circumference $\times$ .0169 = Solidity of sphere.

Cube root of solidity $\times$ 1.2407 = Diameter of sphere.

Diameter of sphere $\times$ .5774 = Side of inscribed cube.

Square root of solidity $\times$ .2821 = Radius.

Square root of solidity $\times$ 1.7725 = Circumference.

Cube of radius $\times$ 4.1888 = Solidity.

Cube root of solidity $\times$ .6204 = Radius.

Cube root of solidity $\times$ 3.8978 = Circumference.

Communism and Socialism.—Communism is a doctrine which would abolish individual rights, including the ownership of property. It began in England and France, but has never made any great progress. Socialism is allied to Communism, but is a milder form. It does not suggest the abolition of individual rights, but to make all rights subordinate to the good of the people. An acceptable definition of either has never been presented, and members of both parties differ materially. Socialism, however, has grown very rapidly, and the Socialistic Party in the United States is frequently successful. Some of our ablest scholars and investigators believe that Socialism will become prevalent, and that it will solve many of our economic problems.

Comparative Population of the United States

Census Year	Population	Preceding Increase Number	Over Census P. C.	Adjusted P. C. of Inc.
1920	105,710,620	13,738,354	14.9	14.9
1910	91,972,266	15,977,691	21.0	21.0
1900	75,994,575	13,046,861	20.7	20.7
1890	62,947,714	12,791,931	25.5	25.5
1880	50,155,783	11,597,412	30.1	26.0
1870	38,558,371	7,115,050	22.6	26.6
1860	31,443,321	8,251,445	35.6	35.6
1850	23,191,876	6,122,423	35.9	35.9
1840	17,069,453	4,203,433	32.7	32.7
1830	12,866,020	3,227,567	33.5	33.5
1820	9,638,453	2,398,572	33.1	33.1

1810	7,239,881	1,931,398	36.4	36.4
1800	5,308,483	1,379,269	35.1	35.1
1790	3,929,214	....	...	...·

Comparative Population of the Large Cities and Towns of the United States

| | | 1920 | |
CLASS OF PLACES		Number of Places	Population
Continental United States		.....	105,710,620
All incorporated places		15,692	63,273,844
Places of 1,000,000 or more		3	10,145,532
Places of 500,000 to 1,000,000 inhabitants		9	6,223,769
Places of 250,000 to 500,000 inhabitants .		13	4,540,838
Places of 100,000 to 250,000 inhabitants .		43	6,519,187
Places of 50,000 to 100,000 inhabitants ..		76	5,265,747
Places of 25,000 to 50,000 inhabitants ...		143	5,075,041
Places of 10,000 to 25,000 inhabitants ...		459	6,942,742
Places of 5,000 to 10,000 inhabitants		721	4,997,794
Places of 2,500 to 5,000		1,320	4,593,953
Places of less than 2,500		12,905	8,969,241

Compass.—The compass was unknown to civilization until the close of the twelfth century, but appears to have been used in China centuries before the European nations were aware of its power. The compass consists of a piece of steel, usually in the form of a needle, which has been magnetized so as to maintain its magnetism indefinitely. It is set on a piece of cork or rests lightly on a pivot, and if allowed to move freely, it will point towards the North Magnetic Pole, the opposite end of the needle indicating the South Magnetic Pole. The needle does not point to the Geographical Pole, but to the North Magnetic Pole, which is some degrees south of the former. The earth is a magnet, and the magnetic needle is influenced by the currents of the earth, and, therefore, points to the North under the influence of these currents. No compass is absolutely correct, for the needle does not always point to the North with a full degree of accuracy. It is subject to variations, which are caused by outside influences, like the presence of metallic substances. Without the compass, navigation would be unsafe, if not impossible, for no mariner, without it, would know the direction he is sailing in at night or during a cloudy day.

Corsets.—The corset, or something similar to what is now worn, appeared in France and Germany in the 13th century, and a 100 years later was introduced into England. The cloth was interwoven with rods of whalebone or steel, but when the price of whalebone increased, other stiffening rods were used.

Cosmetics.—Vaseline, cold cream, and glycerine are perfectly safe to use, although the latter irritates some skins. Most of the cosmetics upon the market, including many of those advertised to produce a good complexion, are practically worthless, and undoubtedly quite a number of them contain poisonous drugs and chemicals. The writer does not recall a cosmetic which contains any virtue not found in cold cream, vaseline, or glycerine. Most cosmetics are made of cold cream or vaseline, highly perfumed, and are claimed to possess special virtues. The only way to obtain a good complexion is to keep the skin in a healthy state by constant bathing and by massage, either with the hands or with a towel, with a moderate use of cold cream or other similar article. Nothing has ever been discovered which will restore the bloom of youth, and all articles advertised for that purpose are practically worthless. If they contain any "bloom," it is in the form of a dye or color. No one should use any concocton or salve other than cold cream, vaseline, glycerine, or an almond preparation, without the advice of a physician.

Cost of the British Royal Family.—The annuities paid by the British people to the Royal family for its support are as follows: The King and Queen, $2,350,000; Queen Alexandra, $350,000; Princess Christian, $30,000; Princess Louise (Duchess of Argyll), $30,000; Duke of Connaught, $125,000; Duchess of Edinburgh, $20,000; Princess Beatrice, $30,000; Duchess of Albany, $30,000; Duchess of Mecklenburg-Strelitz, $15,000; Trustees for King Edward VII's Daughters, $90,000; total, $3,080,000. The King also receives the revenues of the Duchy of Lancaster. During recent years these have amounted to about $500,000 per annum. The Prince of Wales has an income also from the revenues of the Duchy of Cornwall, amounting to about $400,000 per annum. When the Royal children marry dowries are usually provided for them. The last of the children of the late Queen Victoria to marry, Princess Beatrice, received $100,000 as dowry from the British people by Parliamentary grant.

Cotton Gin.—One of the three or four greatest inventions of civilization. It was invented by Eli Whitney in 1793. The machine separates the cotton wool from the seed, and automatically cleans it with great rapidity. Previously, the work was done by hand, a most tedious process.

Cotton Industry.—From 16,000,000 to 17,000,000 bales of cotton are sold each year, each bale weighing about 490 lbs.

Cradle of American Liberty.—A name given to Faneuil Hall, in Boston, Massachusetts, from the fact that many meetings were held here during Revolutionary days for the purpose of declaring the citizens' rights and protesting against the interference of England.

Credit Mobilier.—This consisted of a stock company, organized in 1863, for the purpose of constructing public works, including principally the building of the Union Pacific Railroad. Without going into the merits of the case, it may be said that this organization received much criticism, as it developed that many of the members of Congress were supposed to be connected with it. It is said that some of these members were corrupt and used this organization to feather their nest. It constituted, perhaps, the greatest national scandal, placing under suspicion, as it did, many of our so-called statesmen.

Crusades.—The name of wars carried on at intervals from 1095 to 1270 by the Christian nations of Europe against the Saracens, for the purpose of gaining possession of the Holy Land. There were eight Crusades, and the soldiers who engaged in them wore a cross on their breast or right shoulder as a sign of their religious faith. Hence the name Crusades from the Latin *crux*, cross.

Crust of the Earth.—Very little is known of the interior of the earth, except that it is supposed to be a molten mass. The aggregate thickness of the strata or rock-layers, as far as known, is less than thirty miles.

Daguerreotypes.—Early photography owes its origin to the discovery of the daguerreotype. A plate, made of thin copper or other metal, was covered with a silver preparation. This was placed directly in the camera, and there was no method of transfer, as there is from the ordinary photographic plate, from which innumerable prints may be taken. It went out of common use with the invention of the photographic plates and paper, and with the discovery of instantaneous photography. The taking of the daguerreotype required long exposure, which was decidedly objectionable, and the result was coarse and tame. After taking, the daguerreotype passed through acid solutions for the development and permanency of the picture.

Damage by Lightning.—Statistics vary, but considerably more than 6,000 buildings are injured by lightning every year, causing a loss of about $3,000,000. About 700 people are killed every year, and more than 800 are injured. It is said that lightning kills between 4,000 and 5,000 domestic animals a year, valued at about $130,000.

Deaf and Dumb.—About 90,000 of the inhabitants of the United States are deaf and dumb, more than half of that number being born with this affliction. Of this number about 47,000 are males, and somewhat over 43,000 females.

Deeds.—A deed is an instrument in writing, conveying real estate, with or without buildings upon it, from one party to another. All deeds should be registered. Printed forms, to be filled out, are for sale at stationers. It is better to employ a good lawyer or conveyancer.

Dictionaries.—Probably the first dictionary was produced in China, and was said to contain 40,000 characters. In the 15th and 16th centuries, encyclopedias were published. The first authoritative dictionary was in Latin, and was translated into eight languages about the year 1500. Chamber's Encyclopedia was published in 1728, and Johnson's famous English dictionary in 1755. Webster's American dictionary was first issued in 1828.

Digestibility of Foods.—Apples, sweet, raw, 1 hour, 30 minutes; Asparagus, boiled, 1 h., 30 m.; Beans, boiled, 2 h., 30 m.; Lean beef, roasted, 3 h.; Fresh salted beef, boiled 2 h., 45 m.; Old salted beef, boiled, 6 h.; Beets, boiled, 3h., 45 m.; Bread, fresh, 3h., 30 m.; Cabbage, pickled, 4 h., 30 m.; Celery, boiled, 1 h., 30 m.; Chicken, boiled, 2h.; Chicken, roasted, 4 h.; Cheese, old, 3h., 30 m.; Duck, roasted, 2 h.; Eggs, raw, 2h; Eggs, soft boiled, 3 h.; Eggs, hard boiled, 4 h.; Fish, boiled, 1 h., 30 m.; Fish, fried, 3 h.; Game (most kinds), roasted, 4 h., 15 m.; Liver (calves), fried, 2 h., 30 m.; Lamb, grilled, 2 h., 30 m.; Milk, raw, 3 h., 15 m.; Milk, boiled, 2 h.; Mutton, boiled and broiled, 3 h.; Nuts, 5 h.; Oysters, raw, 2 h., 55 m.; Oysters, stewed, 3 h., 30 m.; Onions, stewed, 3 h., 30 m.; Pork, fat, roasted, 5 h., 15 m.; Pork, salt, boiled, 3 h., 15 m.; Potatoes, fried or baked, 2 h., 30 m.; Rice, boiled, 1 h.; Sausage, grilled, 3 h., 30 m.; Tripe, boiled, 1 h.; Trout, boiled, 1 h., 30 m.; Turkey, roasted, 2 h., 30 m.; Veal, roast or grilled, 5 h.

Distances Between Cities in the United States

(Not air-line distances, but traveling distances.)

(Not air-line distances, but traveling distances.)

From

To	New York Mls.	Chicago Mls.	Philadelphia Mls.	St. Louis Mls.	Boston Mls.	Baltimore Mls.	Cleveland Mls.	Buffalo Mls.	San Francisco Mls.	Pittsburgh Mls.	Cincinnati Mls.	Milwaukee Mls.	New Orleans Mls.	Washington Mls.	Minneapolis Mls.
Atlanta	876	733	785	611	1,106	688	736	919	2,805	805	492	818	496	648	1,153
Baltimore	188	802	97	934	418	....	474	398	3,076	334	593	887	1,184	40	1,222
Boston	217	1,034	321	1,230	....	418	682	499	3,308	674	926	1,119	1,602	458	1,454
Buffalo	442	525	416	731	499	398	183	....	2,799	270	427	610	1,256	438	945
Chicago	912	....	821	284	1,034	802	357	525	2,274	468	298	85	912	790	420
Cincinnati	757	298	666	341	926	593	244	427	2,572	313	....	383	829	553	718
Cleveland	584	357	493	548	682	474	....	183	2,468	135	244	442	1,073	437	777
Denver	1,934	1,022	1,843	916	2,056	1,850	1,379	1,537	1,235	1,490	1,257	1,107	1,347	1,810	884
Detroit	693	272	669	488	750	649	173	251	2,546	321	263	357	1,092	655	692
Galveston	1,792	1,144	1,691	860	2,012	1,594	1,408	1,591	2,457	1,481	1,157	1,229	410	1,554	1,340
Indianapolis	825	183	734	240	965	704	283	466	2,394	381	111	268	888	664	603
Jacksonville, Fla.	983	1,097	892	975	1,213	795	1,085	1,193	3,098	1,057	841	1,182	616	755	1,517
Kansas City	1,342	458	1,251	277	1,466	1,211	755	967	1,981	898	618	543	880	1,171	573
Los Angeles	3,149	2,265	3,058	2,084	3,273	3,018	2,562	2,774	475	2,705	2,425	2,350	2,007	2,978	2,301
Louisville	871	304	780	274	1,040	703	358	541	2,468	427	114	389	778	663	727
Memphis	1,157	527	1,066	311	1,387	969	703	921	2,439	807	494	612	396	875	897
Milwaukee	997	85	906	369	1,119	887	442	610	2,359	553	383	....	997	929	335
Minneapolis	1,332	420	1,241	586	1,454	1,222	777	945	2,096	888	718	335	1,285	1,210	....
Montreal	386	841	477	1,051	330	574	623	434	3,115	704	826	925	1,655	614	1,125
New Orleans	1,372	912	1,281	699	1,602	1,184	1,073	1,256	2,482	1,142	829	997	....	1,144	1,285
New York	....	912	91	1,065	217	188	473	442	3,186	444	757	997	1,372	228	1,332
Omaha	1,405	493	1,314	413	1,527	1,295	584	1,018	1,781	961	666	573	1,080	1,283	381
Philadelphia	91	821	....	974	321	97	493	416	3,095	353	666	906	1,281	137	1,241
Pittsburgh	444	468	353	621	674	334	135	270	2,742	....	313	553	1,142	302	888
Portland, Ore.	3,204	2,292	3,113	2,212	3,326	3,094	2,649	2,817	772	2,760	2,590	2,378	2,746	3,082	2,042
Quebec	530	1,013	621	1,343	402	718	795	731	3,287	876	1,039	1,098	1,827	786	1,433
St. Louis	1,065	284	974	....	1,230	934	548	731	2,194	621	341	369	699	894	586
San Francisco	3,186	2,274	3,095	2,194	3,308	3,076	2,631	2,799	....	2,742	2,572	2,359	2,482	3,064	2,096
Seattle	3,151	2,239	3,060	2,332	3,273	2,941	2,596	2,764	957	2,707	2,537	2,154	2,931	3,029	1,818
Washington	228	790	137	894	458	40	437	438	3,064	302	553	875	1,144	....	1,210

Diving Bells.— The diving bell is simply a covering made of metal, which is securely fastened to a water-proof suit, the diving bell itself being an enclosure for the head. The diver dons his suit, the neck of which has a collar in the form of a screw. The diving bell is placed over his head and screwed on. It is connected with a rubber pipe, through which air is forced by an air pump, the air escaping through a valve in the belt itself. If properly constructed and manipulated, one may remain under water for considerable time, although he is likely to be uncomfortable until he becomes used to it. It was invented about 1715.

Drama.—From June 1919 to June 1920 there were produced 30 musical comedies, 38 dramas of serious, romantic, or sentimental nature, 11 melodramas, 35 comedies, 5 tragedies, 10 farces, and 13 revues, approximating 150 in all.

Drugs.—The safest and best rule to follow is never to take any drug without the advice of a physician. Drugs have their place, and without drugs many diseases would be incurable. But drugs taken promiscuously derange the system and give but temporary relief. Hundreds of thousands of people have contracted chronic ailments from drug-taking. Headache powders, cough mixtures, sleeping potions, and practically all of the advertised remedies should be strenuously avoided, notwithstanding that some of them are pure and would be efficacious if administered intelligently. Because one particular drug or medicine benefits a certain person should not be considered as evidence that it will aid another. The habit of borrowing prescriptions is dangerous. The intelligent physician writes a prescription, which will benefit his patient, and the same prescription would be of no benefit, and might be of positive injury, to another. Many of the testimonials given to patent medicines are genuine and are written by honest persons. The effect of many of the advertised nostrums is to give immediate or transient relief. They stimulate the system, and may make it feel better for a short time, but re-action is likely to set in, and the taker of them is worse off than he was in the first place.

Dying Sayings, Real or Traditional.—Addison. " See how a Christian dies ! " or, " See in what a peace a Christian can die ! "

Anaxagoras. " Give the boys a holiday."

Byron. " I must sleep now."

Cæsar (Julius). " Et tu, Brute ! "

Charlemagne. " Lord, into Thy hands I commend my spirit ! "

Charles II (of England). " Don't let poor Nelly starve ! "

Chesterfield. " Give Day Rolles a chair."

Cromwell. " My desire is to make what haste I may to be gone."

Franklin. "A dying man can do nothing easy."

Goethe. "More light!"

Hobbes. "Now I am about to take my last voyage—a great leap in the dark."

James V (of Scotland). "It came with a lass, and will go with a lass."

Jesus Christ. "It is finished!"

Knox. "Now it is come."

Mahomet. "Oh Allah, be it so! Henceforth among the glorious host of Paradise."

Mirabeau. "Let me die to the sounds of delicious music."

Napoleon I. "Mon Dieu! La nation Française! Fête d'armée."

Napoleon III. "Were you at Sedan?"

Nelson. "I thank God I have done my duty."

Rabelais. "Let down the curtain, the farce is over."

Scott, Sir Walter. "God bless you all!"

Sidney, Algernon. "I know that my Redeemer liveth. I die for the good old cause."

Socrates. "Crito, we owe a cock to Aesculapius."

Talma. "The worst is, I cannot see."

Tasso. "Lord, into Thy hands I commend my spirit!"

Vespasian. "A king should die standing."

William III of England. "Can this last long?"

Wolfe, General. "What! do they run already? Then I die happy."
—Brewer's "Reader's Handbook."

Dynamite.—This is one of the strongest explosives, and is used for blasting, and even for guns, although it has not, as yet, been successful for the firing of projectiles. It consists of infusorial and porcelain earth, mixed with coal dust and siliceous ashes, saturated with about three times its weight of nitro-glycerine. It is of a grayish-brown or reddish color, damp, and greasy. It has an explosive power nearly eight times greater than that of gun powder. It is dangerous to make, because the nitro-glycerine which it contains will explode if not handled carefully.

Earth Facts

The distance from the surface of the earth to its center is estimated to be 20,926,202 feet; or about 3,963, miles; and the distance from the poles to the center of the earth is 20,854,895 feet, or about 3,951 miles. One degree of latitude at the equator is about 68.7 miles, and at the poles about 69½ miles.

The circumference at the equator measures 24,902 statute miles.

The total area of the earth is 196,940,000 statute square miles, and its volume is 259,880 million cubic miles.

The land area of the earth covers 56,255,000 square miles.

The water area covers 140,295,000 square miles, or about 71 per cent. of the total surface of the earth.

There are three great oceans: the Atlantic, 41,321,000 square miles; the Pacific, 68,634,000 square miles; the Indian, 29,430,000 square miles. Lake and river surface on land is about 1,000,000 square miles; islands in the seas about 1,910,000 square miles.

The mean height of the land has been estimated at 2,300 feet, and the mean depth of the sea 12,600 feet. The highest mountain (Mt. Everest) is 29,000 feet high, and the greatest depth of the ocean, off Mindanao, Philippine Islands, is 32,088 feet.

The North American continent has an area of 8,589,257 square miles, with exceeding 150,-000,000 inhabitants, or 16.3 to the square mile.

The South American continent has an area of 7,570,015 square miles, with 56,337,775 inhabitants, or 7.4 per square mile.

Europe has an area of about 3,872,561 square miles, with a population of 464,681,000, or about 120 per square mile.

Africa has an area of 11,622,619 square miles, and a population of about 142,751,000, or 12.3 to the square mile.

Asia has an area of 17,206,000 square miles, with a population estimated at about 872,522,-000 or 50.7 to the square mile.

Australasia has an area of 3,312,613 square miles, with a population of 16,228,591, or about 4.9 to the square mile.

Total population of the earth is about 1,702,-520,000, or about 29.6 to the square mile. At present rate of increase there will be about 4,000,000,000 in 2014.

It is estimated that the surface of the earth is divided into somewhat more than 29,000,000 square miles of fertile soil, about 14,000,000 square miles of steppe, a little more than 4,861,000 square miles of desert, with the polar regions occupying 6,970,000 square miles of land, most of which is covered with ice.

At the time of Emperor Augustus, there were said to be between 54,000,000 and 55,-000,000 people upon the earth, but as the earth undoubtedly supported millions of inhabitants unknown to civilization, these figures are of little consequence.

The greatest measured depth of the Atlantic Ocean is a little over 27,000 feet; a depth of 32,000 feet has been found in the Pacific Ocean; 18,582 feet in the Indian Ocean.

Earthquakes.—The earthquake is caused, undoubtedly, by the cooling of the earth. The interior of the earth is a molten mass of fire and is slowly cooling. As it cools, it contracts, and if the contraction is near the surface of the earth, the surface is rocked and crevices may open, doing considerable damage, although most earthquakes cause but slight shocks and injure no one. Earthquakes appear principally in or near the tropics, but are occasionally felt all over the temperature zones. Earthquakes appear to have belts, and there is little to be feared from them outside of these territories.

Earthquake Areas of the Earth

Major de Montessus de Balore has compiled a catalogue of 130,000 shocks, and this indicates with scientific accuracy how the symptoms of seismic activity are manifested. The period of observation includes generally the last fifty years; but there is no reason to suppose that a longer time would materially affect the proportionate numbers.

Area	Earth-quakes	Area	Earth-quakes
Scandinavia	646	Africa	179
British Isles	1,139	Atlantic islands....	1,704
France	2,793	United States, Pacific coast........	4,467
Spain and Portugal	2,656		
Switzerland	3,895	Atlantic coast......	937
Italy	27,672	Mexico	5,586
Holland and North Germany	2,326	Central America...	2,739
Sicily	4,331	West Indies.......	2,561
Greece	10,306	South America.....	8,081
Russia	258	Java	2,155
Asia Minor	4,451	Australia and Tasmania	83
India	813	New Zealand......	1,925
Japan	27,562		

The most shaken countries of the world are Italy, Japan, Greece, South America (the Pacific coast), Java, Sicily, and Asia Minor. The lands most free from these convulsions are Africa, Australia, Russia, Siberia, Scandinavia, and Canada. As a rule, where earthquakes are most frequent they are most severe. But to this general statement there are exceptions—Indian shocks, though less numerous, being often very disastrous. Loss of life in many cases depends, however, on density of population rather than on the intensity of the earth movement. Numerically, also, France has registered more seismic tremors than Spain and Portugal, but France in historic times has experienced no earthquake disaster approaching the havoc wrought by the one calamity at Lisbon.

Electrical and Other Beautifiers.—So far as is known to the writer, none of these contrivances or concoctions possess any merit, other than what may be obtained by ordinary massage or rubbing. Electricity, as a medicinal agent, is rapidly going out of use, as it has been proved that it has very little effect, except in special cases. The reader is advised against the purchase of any electrical appliance for beautifying or other purposes without the advice of a physician.

Electricity.—This peculiar and all-powerful energy has never been analyzed, and no one knows exactly what it is. It is produced by friction, either mechanically or by chemicals.

It is transmitted through wires or other metallic conductors. Electricity is usually produced mechanically by what is known as the dynamo, but can be made chemically by the use of galvanic batteries. The former, however, is much more economical. Electricity and magnetism are closely allied, and yet they are commercially different.

Embezzlement. — Embezzlement in the United States amounts to about $10,000,000 annually, the majority of embezzlers stealing the money for gambling in stocks, and not on account of increased personal expenses or desire to live beyond their means.

Errors of History

The following list of "Curious Errors of History" is taken from Conklin's "Vest Pocket Argument Settler":

William Tell was a myth.

Coriolanus never allowed his mother to intercede for Rome.

Blondel, the harper, did not discover the prison in which Richard I was confined.

Nero was not a monster; he did not kill his mother nor fiddle over burning Rome.

Alfred never allowed the cakes to burn, nor ventured into the Danish camp disguised as a minstrel.

Fair Rosamond was not poisoned by Queen

Eleanor, but died in the odor of sanctity in the convent of Godstow.

The Duke of Wellington, at Waterloo, never uttered the famous words, " Up, Guards, and at them ! "

Charles Kingsley gave up his chair of modern history at Oxford because he said he considered history " largely a lie."

Chemists have proved that vinegar will not dissolve pearls nor cleave rocks, in spite of the fabled exploits of Cleopatra and Hannibal.

Charles IX did not fire upon the Huguenots with an arquebus from the window of the Louvre during the massacre of St. Bartholomew.

The siege of Troy is largely a myth, even according to Homer's own account. Helen must have been 60 years old when Paris fell in love with her.

The crew of *Le Vengeur*, instead of going down with the cry of " Vive la République ! " shrieked for help.

The number of Xerxes's army has been grossly exaggerated, and it was not stopped at Thermoyplæ by 300 Spartans, but 7,000. or even, as some authorities compute, 12,000.

The Abbé Edgeworth frankly acknowledged to Lord Holland that he had never made the famous invocation to Louis XVI on the scaffold : " Son of St. Louis, ascend to heaven."

Philip VI, flying from the field of Crécy,

and challenged late at night before the gates of the castle of Blois, did not cry out, " It is the fortune of France." What he really said was: " Open, open; it is the unfortunate king of France."

Voltaire, on being asked where he had heard the story that when the French became masters of Constantinople in 1204 they danced with the women in the sanctuary of the Church of Santa Sophia, replied calmly: " Nowhere; it is a frolic of my imagination."

There is no evidence that Romulus ever lived, that Tarquin outraged Lucretia, that Brutus shammed idiocy and condemned his sons to death, that Mucius Scaevola thrust his hand into the fire, that Cloelia swam the Tiber, that Horatius defended a bridge against an army.

Esperanto.—Some years ago several educators attempted to develop an international language, to be used by the speaking and writing world at large. This auxiliary language is made from the roots of other languages, including the Latin. Its pronounciation is wholly phonetic. Theoretically, at least, it has tremendous advantages, for should it be generally adopted by the civilized nations, who would, undoubtedly, retain their native language, there would be a common basis for international communication, and people could get together socially and otherwise without being linguists. The growth of

Esperanto is slow, although encouraged by many educators. It is problematical whether or not it will make sufficient strides to be generally accepted. It has its faults, and it is quite probable that, if an international language, or auxiliary language, is to be obtained, some other form of common speech will take its place; or, Esperanto may be changed, modified, or enlarged, so as to be more acceptable. Civilization, however, demands a universal language, one which will eventually take the place of all modern languages, the present languages to be relegated to the dead class; but natural conditions, association, and patriotism, or the semblance of them, will, undoubtedly, make it extremely difficult to introduce any other form of speech, or of writing, which would interfere with native tongues.

Failures

During 1920, there were 8,881 commercial failures in the United States, with total assets of $195,504,843 and liabilities of $295,121,805. These were divided as follows: 2,635 in manufacturing; 5,532 in trading; and 714 in other commercial enterprises.

During 1919, there were 6,451 commercial failures in the United States, with total assets of $67,037,843 and liabilities of $113,291,237. These were divided as follows: 1,865 in manufacturing; 4,013 in trading; and 573 in other commercial enterprises.

In 1918 there were 9,982 commercial failures, with total assets of $101,637,798 and liabilities of $163,019,979. These were divided as follows: 2,766 in manufacturing; 6,494 in trading; and 722 in other commercial enterprises.

The following table gives the bank failures in the United States between 1893 and 1920.

YEAR.		TOTAL.		NATIONAL.
	No.	Liab., Dols.	No.	Liab., Dols.
1920	119	50,708,300	10	3,350,000
1919	50	16,520,862	4	1,850,000
1918	20	5,131,887	0	None.
1917	42	18,451,964	4	3,700,000
1916	50	10,396,779	8	1,755,000
1915	133	37,223,234	18	13,649,000
1913	120	31,546,314	7	5,197,336
1912	79	24,219,522	4	8,313,000
1911	107	25,511,606	3	1,250,000
1910	119	41,097,255	10	4,284,482
1909	80	24,677,128	11	4,109,224
1908	180	123,126,956	31	48,388,000
1907	132	233,325,972	12	12,533,000
1906	58	18,805,380	8	1,490,966
1905	78	20,227,155	16	4,198,348
1904	99	28,158,811	24	10,257,223
1903	121	29,685,766	12	5,735,477
1902	63	10,969,072	2	420,617
1901	74	18,018,774	9	5,666,231
1900	58	14,456,563	5	1,312,721
1899	55	27,116,790	10	7,106,567
1898	80	18,395,094	11	4,102,290
1897	171	28,249,700	28	5,977,421
1896	198	50,718,915	34	22,674,512
1895	132	20,710,210	34	5,863,842
1894	125	125,666,035	18	4,803,616
1893	642	210,998,808	161	67,673,894

It will be noted that, with the stricter control of banks by the Federal and State governments, losses by bank failures are greatly diminishing.

Famous Diamonds.—The following is a list
of the most famous diamonds of the world:
(1) The Braganza, (2) the Dudley, (3) the
Florentine, (4) the Great Mogul, (5) the
Hope, (6) the Koh-i-nur, (7) the Nassac, (8)
the Orloff, (9) the Pigott, (10) the Pitt or
Regent, (11) the Sancy, (12) the Shah, (13)
the Star of the South.

Farm Production

The figures are given in round numbers:
Animals, over 206,000,000, valued at over $5,-
000,000,000; Apples, over 147,000,000 bushels,
valued at over $83,000,000; Apricots, over 4,-
000,000 bushels, valued at over $2,800,000;
Beans (Dry), over 11,200,000 bushels, valued
at about $22,000,000; Bees, over 3,445,000
swarms, valued at over $10,300,000; Broom
Corn, over 78,900,000 pounds, valued at over
$5,130,000; Butter, over 531,000,000 pounds,
valued at over $113,000,000; Cereals, over 4,-
280,000,000 bushels, valued at over $2,694,000,-
000; Cheese, over 317,000,000 pounds, valued
at over $28,600,000; Chicory, about 21,500,000
pounds, valued at over $73,000; Cotton, over
8,000,000,000 pounds, valued at over $730,000,-
000; Cotton Seed, over 6,900,000 tons, valued
at over $127,400,000; Flaxseed, over 19,300,000
bushels, valued at over $35,000,000; Flowers,
plants, valued at over $18,700,000; Forest Pro-
ducts, valued at over $109,800,000; Fruits,
(small), valued at over $29,900,000; Fruits,

(subtropical), valued at over $24,700,000; Grapes, over 2,500,000,000 pounds, valued at over $22,000,000; Hay, about 55,000,000 tons, valued at over $784,900,000; Hemp, over 11,-750,000 pounds, valued at over $540,000; Honey, over 62,800,000 pounds, valued at over $6,600,000; Hops, over 40,700,000 pounds, valued at over $7,800,000; Milk, over 7,265,-000,000 gallons; Molasses, over 6,300,000 gallons, valued at over $788,000; Nursery products, valued at over $10,100,000; Nuts, valued at over $4,400,000; Onions, over 11,700,000 bushels, valued at over $6,600,000; Orchard products, over 216,000,000 bushels, valued at over $140,800,000; Peaches, over 35,400,000 bushels, valued at over $28,700,000; Peanuts, over 19,400,000 bushels, valued at over $18,-200,000; Pears, over 8,800,000 bushels, valued at over $7,900,000; Peas, dry, over 7,500,000 bushels, valued at over $11,100,000; Plums, and Prunes, over 15,400,000 bushels, valued at about $10,300,000; Potatoes (Irish), about 292,800,000 bushels, valued at over $233,700,-000; Potatoes (Sweet), over 59,200,000 bushels, valued at over $35,300,000; Rice, over 22,-900,000 bushels, valued at over $18,200,000; Seeds, Clover, over 1,000,000 bushels, valued at over $6,900,000; Seeds, Grass, over 3,500,-000 bushels, valued at over $2,800,000; Sugar, Beet, about 12,300,000,000 pounds, valued at over $23,800,000; Sugar, Cane, over 1,100,000 tons, valued at over $28,800,000; Sugar, Maple, over 11,900,000 pounds, valued at over $1,000,000; Syrup, Cane, over 12,200,000 gallans, valued at about $4,300,000; Syrup, Maple, over 2,000,000 gallons, valued at over $1,500,-000; Syrup, Sorghum, over 16,900,000 gallons, valued at over $5,200,000; Tobacco, over 900,-100,000 pounds, valued at over $85,200,000; Vegetables (miscellaneous), valued at over $113,600,000; Wool, over 318,500,000 pounds, valued at over $66,500,000.

First Trans-Atlantic Steamship.—The " Savannah," a vessel of only 350 tons, and measuring 100 feet, was the first steamship to cross the Atlantic Ocean. She was launched in New York in 1818. She was propelled with paddles and ship-rigged. She crossed the Atlantic in 26 days, her engine being used only 16 days. The rest of the time she was under sail.

Flour Industry.—There are nearly 12,000 flour mills in the United States, requiring a capital of about $350,000,000. These mills use nearly $770,000,000 worth of material a year, and pay salaries and wages of about $35,000,-000. The annual market value of the flour milled annually is nearly $900,000,000.

Food Nutriment.—On a basis of 1,000 parts, the nutriment value of foods may be listed as follows:

Cucumber	25	Cherries	250
Melons	30	Veal	250
Turnips	42	Beef	260

Milk	72	Potatoes	260
Cabbage	73	Apricots	260
Carrots	98	Grapes	270
White of egg	140	Chicken	270
Pears	160	Plums	290
Apples	170	Mutton	290
Haddock	180	Oats	742
Gooseberries	190	Rye	792
Peaches	200	Rice	880
Codfish	210	Barley	920
Pork	240	Wheat	950

Forests.—Original forests in the United States covered about 822,000,000 acres and contained 5,200,000,000,000 board feet of lumber. On June 30, 1920 there were left 463,000,000 acres of forest land, containing 2,214,000,000,-000 board feet. 180,299,776 acres are owned by the government. Timber consumed is more than four times the annual growth.

Foretelling the Weather

Several years ago the United States Government established a Weather Bureau and placed it in charge of scientific men and observers who were expert in this direction. Weather Bureau stations are maintained throughout the United States, and each station communicates daily with the head office at Washington. By following the law of averages, by the use of the barometer and other instruments, by scientific research and experiment, and because of the receipt of hourly or daily reports,

the Weather Bureau experts are able to foretell the weather with a considerable degree of
accuracy. Practically all of the great storms,
tornadoes, and hurricanes are announced in
advance. While this science is still in its in-
fancy, it has made rapid strides, and each year
shows much improvement in the result.
There are a few simple rules, which may be
used for foretelling the weather, if one pos-
sesses a barometer.

The rapid rise of the barometer indicates
unsettled weather. The gradual rise foretells
settled weather.

When the air is dry and cold, a rising barometer indicates wind from the north; and if it
has been raining, better weather may occur.

When the air is moist and at a low temperature, a rising barometer may foretell wind and
rain from the north.

When there is a northerly wind, and the
barometer falls rapidly, there is likely to be a
storm with snow in winter, and heavy rain or
hail in summer.

When the air is dry and the temperature
seasonable, a steady barometer indicates a
continuance of fine weather.

A rapidly falling barometer may foretell
stormy weather.

When the wind is westerly, a rapid fall may
precede a storm coming from the north.

When the wind is southerly, a rise in the
barometer may precede fine weather.

When there is much moisture in the air and considerable heat, a falling barometer may indicate that a wind and rain storm is coming from the south.

When the air is dry and cold in winter a falling barometer may indicate snow. When the weather is calm and warm, a falling barometer may be taken to mean rain or squally weather.

Freemasonry.—Its origin is unknown, but it is very ancient. It has been traced to the Knights Templars, to the Crusaders, and others. It is said that the workmen upon Solomon's Temple were Masons and that Masonry was the original trade union or protective association for workmen, each workman by signs being able to prove that he had reached a certain stage of proficiency; but this has not been substantiated. Some authorities state that Masonry was introduced into England in 674 A. D. The first record of the establishment of a Grand Lodge was at York in 926. Freemasonry was introduced into France in 1725, and into America in 1730. Freemasons are found throughout the entire world, there being more than a million of them in the United States and Canada. Other fraternal or mystic orders, known as Odd Fellows, Knights of Pythias, Red Men, etc., are in purpose similar to Masons, and most of them were founded upon Masonry, Masonry ante-dating all of them.

French Academy.—Founded by Cardinal Richelieu in 1635. It has a membership of forty, known as the " Forty Immortals." Its principal object is to prepare a dictionary of the French language and to keep the Gallic tongue pure and capable of treating the arts and sciences. The first dictionary appeared in 1694. The Academy has been very severely criticised, especially in the selection of its members, many well-known men of letters having failed to be elected.

Gold in California.—John W. Marshall, in 1848, in connection with a man named Sutter, maintained a mill in California. Accidentally he picked up a small piece of metal which he discovered to be gold, and immediately the gold fever became epidemic, and California was overrun with gold miners.

Government

The Constitution of the United States is the basic law of the country, and all other laws and statutes are framed in a similar manner, each State, county, town, and city having its own laws or statutes.

Government, including that of the United States, is divided into three distinctive departments: Executive, Legislative, and Judicial.

The Executive head is known as President, Governor, Mayor, etc., and it is his duty to execute the laws.

The Legislative department is usually subdivided into two bodies,—a Senate or Upper House and a House of Representatives or Lower House. State Governments are formed similar to that of the National Government, the Upper House being known as the Senate, and the Lower House as the House of Representatives or Assembly. Most bills are presented to the Lower House, and do not become laws until they pass both the Upper and Lower Houses.

The Legislative authority of a city is usually vested in a board of Aldermen and a Council or Common Council, but occasionally there is only one legislative body, known as a Council.

The Commission Form of Government is becoming somewhat prevalent. It consists of a committee elected by the citizens, who have absolute control of the government, and this body is both executive and judicial.

The Judicial department consists of several courts: first, the Supreme Court, and a lower court, usually known as the Superior Court, and District or Police Courts. Ordinary cases are tried by the Police or District Courts and may be appealed to the Superior Court and even to the Supreme Court. Besides these courts there are several courts known as Probate Court, Court of Equity, etc. The Supreme Court, as a rule, deals only with questions at law, and few cases reach it which have not been appealed from the lower courts.

Grain Industry.—There was raised in the United States during 1920 over 3,216,000,000 bushels of Indian corn, about 750,000,000 bushels of wheat, 1,444,000,000 bushels of oats, about 191,000,000 bushels of barley, about 77,-000,000 bushels of rye, and about 19,000,-000 bushels of buckwheat.

Gravity.—The force of gravity, unscientifically speaking, is the influence which one body has upon another, commonly known as attraction. All material substances attempt to draw others to them, and the larger the substance, the greater its attractiveness or drawing power. The earth, being larger than anything near it, draws everything to it. A ball thrown into the air returns to the earth as soon as the force which propelled it upward is exhausted. If the ball were larger than the earth, the earth would move toward the ball, or rather each would move toward the other, but the smaller body would go the greater distance. The entire universe would, undoubtedly, come together in one solid mass if the bodies were not held apart by laws and energies, which are not yet fully understood by men. Sir Isaac Newton discovered the action of gravity, but no one knows exactly what it is.

Great American Inventions

The following list of fifteen great American

inventions is taken from Killikelly's " Curious Questions ":

(1) The Cotton Gin.
(2) The Planting Machine.
(3) The Grass Mower and Reaper.
(4) The Rotary Printing-Press.
(5) Steam Navigation.
(6) The Hot-Air Engine.
(7) The Sewing-Machine.
(8) The India-Rubber Industry.
(9) The Machine Manufacture of Horse-shoes.
(10) The Sand-Blast for Carving.
(11) The Gauge Lathe.
(12) The Grain Elevator.
(13) Artificial Ice-Making on Large Scale.
(14) The Electric Magnet and Its Practical Application.
(15) The Telephone.

" Great Eastern."—The " Great Eastern " was, in her time, the largest vessel in the world, but would be considered small compared with the giant ocean liners of to-day. She was built in London and launched in 1858. She cost $300,000. She had a length of 680 ft., breadth of 82½ ft., or 118 ft. including the paddle boxes, and a height of 58 ft. Her motive power consisted of eight engines with a total of 11,000 horse power. She was slow and unwieldy, and was not a success except for the laying of the Atlantic cable.

Great Libraries.—The Congressional Library, Washington, contains 2,615,000 volumes; Boston Public Library, 1,174,000; New York Public Library, 2,289,000; Harvard University Library, 1,200,000; New York State Library, 506,000; Yale University Library, 800,000; Bibliothèque nationale, Paris, 2,600,-000; British Museum, London, 2,000,000; Imper. publicnaja biblioteka, St. Petersburg, 1,330,000; Königliche Bibliothek, Berlin, 1,-200,000; Kön. Hof-u. Staatsbibliothek, Munich, 1,000,000; K. u. k. Hofbibliothek, Vienna, 900,000.

Great Tunnels.—The Alberg tunnel under the Alps is 6¾ miles long. The Gunnison tunnel in Colorado is 6 miles long. The Hoosac tunnel in Massachusetts is 4¾ miles long. The Mont Cenis in Italy and France is 8 miles long. The New Croton water tunnel in New York is 33⅛ miles long. The Otira in New Zealand is 5 1-3 miles long. The tunnel which drains the Freiberg mines, Saxony, is 31½ miles long.

The St. Clair tunnel, connecting Sarnia, Ont., with Port Huron, Mich., is 2 miles long. The St. Gothard tunnel in the Alps is 9 1-3 miles long. The Strawberry tunnel in the Wasatch Mountains is 50 miles long.

Hair Growers.—Notwithstanding the claims made by advertisers of patent nostrums, the writer has not as yet heard of a preparation or treatment which will restore hair after the hair cells are dead. It appears to be utterly impossible to grow hair upon a bald head, or upon a bald spot, unless the roots of the hair remain, notwithstanding the claims made by sellers of hair tonics. Falling hair may be prevented in many cases by the use of a good hair tonic, but as different people require different preparations, it is inadvisable to give any prescription here. A physician should be consulted, and a prescription obtained from him, adapted to conditions. Many of the advertised hair tonics contain lead and other poisonous drugs. So far as is known, there is not a preparation or contrivance of any kind which will restore gray hair to its former color. All nostrums advertised to do it are simply hair dyes. The medical profession has not discovered a method of preventing gray hair. Most of the advertised hair dyes contain lead and other poisons, and are dangerous to use, and the dyeing of the hair is not to be recommended even though a nonpoisonous dye is used. As the dye can only cover the hair in sight, it must be used constantly, or each separate hair will be of two colors.

Half-Century of Life.—A French statistician states that a man fifty years of age has spent 6000 days in sleep, has worked 6500 days; walked 800 days; enjoyed some amusement 4000 days; spent 1500 days in bed; and was sick 500 days. He further estimates that this man has eaten 17,000 pounds of bread:

16,000 pounds of meat; 4600 pounds of vegetables, eggs, and fish; and has drank 7000 gallons of liquid.

Hawaii.—The Hawaiian Islands have a total area of 6,449 square miles, and a population of about 255,000. The climate is semitropical, and pineapple growing and sugar making are the principal industries.

Hay Industry.—Over 48,000,000 acres are devoted to hay, producing nearly 4,500,000 tons, of a value not far from $50,000,000 a year.

Health.—Ninety per cent. of common ailments, and fully one-half of serious diseases, may be prevented if one gives a reasonable amount of attention to the care of his health. It would be out of place to present, in this book, any rules or regulations for the maintenance of health, assuming that it is possible to do so. Any good physician is competent to advise in the majority of cases, and will prescribe beneficial exercise and proper food. Most of us eat too much, and exercise too little. The province of the physician is as much to keep people well as it is to cure them. Good sense and economy suggest that a physician be consulted at least once a year, even by those in apparent health. So-called "doctors' books" should be avoided, unless recommended by regular practitioners..

Historical Data

STATE OR TERRITORY	Admitted to the Union	Population, 1920	Area, Sq. M.	Settled at	Date	By whom	Electoral vote
Alabama	Dec. 14, 1819	2,348,174	51,279	Mobile	1702	French	12
Alaska Territory	July 27, 1868	55,036	590,884	Sitka	1801	Russians	—
Arizona	Feb. 14, 1912	334,162	113,810	Tucson	1580	Spaniards	3
Arkansas	June 15, 1836	1,752,204	52,525	Arkansas Post	1685	French	9
California	Sept. 9, 1850	3,426,861	155,652	San Diego	1769	Spaniards	13
Colorado	Aug. 1, 1876	939,629	103,658	Near Denver	1858	Americans	6
CONNECTICUT	Jan. 9, 1788	1,380,631	4,820	Windsor	1635	Puritans	7
DELAWARE	Dec. 7, 1787	223,003	1,965	Cape Henlopen	1627	Swedes	3
District of Columbia		437,571	60			English	..
Florida	March 3, 1845	968,470	54,861	St. Augustine	1565	Spaniards	6
GEORGIA	Jan. 2, 1788	2,895,832	58,725	Savannah	1733	English	14
Hawaii	April 30, 1900	255,912	6,449				..
Idaho	July 3, 1890	431,866	83,354	Coeur d'Alene	1842	Americans	4
Illinois	Dec. 3, 1818	6,485,280	56,043	Kaskaskia	1720	French	29
Indiana	Dec. 11, 1816	2,930,390	36,045	Vincennes	1730	French	15
Iowa	Dec. 28, 1846	2,404,021	55,586	Burlington	1788	French	13
Kansas	Jan. 29, 1861	1,769,257	81,774		1831	Americans	10
Kentucky	June 1, 1792	2,416,630	40,181	Lexington	1765	From Va.	13
Louisiana	April 30, 1812	1,798,509	45,409	Iberville	1699	French	10
Maine	March 15, 1820	768,014	29,895	Bristol	1624	English	6
MARYLAND	April 28, 1788	1,449,661	9,941	St. Mary's	1634	English	8
MASSACHUSETTS	Feb. 6, 1788	3,852,356	8,039	Plymouth	1620	Puritans	18
Michigan	Jan. 26, 1837	3,668,412	57,480	Near Detroit	1650	French	15
Minnesota	May 11, 1858	2,387,125	80,858	St. Peter's R.	1805	Americans	12
Mississippi	Dec. 10, 1817	1,790,618	46,362	Natchez	1716	From S. C.	10
Missouri	Aug. 10, 1821	3,404,055	68,727	St. Louis	1764	French	18
Montana	Nov. 8, 1889	548,889	146,131		1809	Americans	4

Historical Data

State or Territory	Admitted to the Union	Population, 1920	Area, Sq. M.	Settled at	Date	By whom	Electoral vote
Nebraska	March 1, 1867	1,296,372	76,808	Bellevue	1847	Americans	8
Nevada	Oct. 31, 1864	77,407	109,821	Genoa	1850	Americans	3
NEW HAMPSHIRE	June 21, 1788	443,083	9,031	Dov. & Portsmouth	1623	Puritans	4
NEW JERSEY	Dec. 18, 1787	3,155,900	7,514	Bergen	1620	Swedes	14
New Mexico	Jan. 6, 1912	360,350	122,503	Santa Fe	1537	Spaniards	3
NEW YORK	July 26, 1788	10,385,227	47,654	Manhattan Island	1614	Dutch	45
NORTH CAROLINA	Nov. 21, 1789	2,559,123	48,740	Albemarle	1650	English	12
North Dakota	Nov. 2, 1889	646,872	70,183	Pembina	1780	French	5
Ohio	Feb. 19, 1803	5,759,394	40,740	Marietta	1788	Americans	24
Oklahoma	Nov. 16, 1907	2,028,283	69,414		1889	Americans	10
Oregon	Feb. 14, 1859	783,389	95,607	Astoria	1810	Americans	5
PENNSYLVANIA	Dec. 12, 1787	8,720,017	44,832	Delaware R.	1682	English	38
Philippines	Nov. 28, 1898	10,350,640	115,026	Manila	1570	Spaniards	..
Porto Rico	Aug. 12, 1898	1,299,809	3,435	Caparra	1510	Spaniards	..
RHODE ISLAND	May 29, 1790	604,397	1,087	Providence	1636	English	5
SOUTH CAROLINA	May 23, 1788	1,683,724	30,495	Port Royal	1670	Huguenots	9
South Dakota	Nov. 2, 1889	636,547	76,868	Sioux Falls	1856	Americans	5
Tennessee	June 1, 1796	2,337,885	41,687	Ft. Loudon	1757	English	12
Texas	Dec. 29, 1845	4,663,228	262,398	Matagorda R.	1686	French	20
Utah	Jan. 4, 1896	449,396	82,184	Salt Lake City	1847	Americans	4
Vermont	March 4, 1791	352,428	9,124	Ft. Dummer	1764	English	4
VIRGINIA	June 26, 1788	2,309,187	40,262	Jamestown	1607	English	12
Washington	Nov. 11, 1889	1,356,621	66,836	Astoria	1811	Americans	7
West Virginia	June 20, 1863	1,463,701	24,022	Wheeling	1774	Americans	8
Wisconsin	May 20, 1848	2,632,067	55,256	Green Bay	1670	French	13
Wyoming	July 11, 1890	194,402	97,548	Ft. Laramie	1884	Americans	3

Holy Grail.—One of the leading themes of medieval romance. It centers around the cup which was used by Christ at the last supper.

Household Weights.—Ten eggs of ordinary size weigh one pound. Sugar—One pint of sugar weighs twelve ounces. Two teacups (well-heaped) of sugar weigh one pound. One and one-third pints of powdered sugar weigh one pound. One pint of the best brown sugar weighs thirteen ounces. Two teacups (level full) of granulated sugar weigh one pound. One tablespoon (heaped) of granulated, or best brown, sugar weighs one ounce. Two and three-quarters teacups (level) of powdered sugar weigh one pound. Two and one-half teacups (level) of best brown sugar weigh one pound. Two tablespoonfuls of powdered sugar or flour weigh one ounce. One pint (heaped) of granulated sugar weighs fourteen ounces.

How to Become a Voter.—Every natural-born citizen of the United States, and all naturalized citizens, are, at the age of 21 years, entitled to vote for all local, State, and National officials; but before doing so, they must be registered. Registration days are appointed, and notices of them are posted in prominent places, and appear in the local newspapers. To become a voter, a citizen must appear at place of registration and answer certain simple questions. Any town or city clerk, attorney at law, or official will properly direct the citizen.

Industrial Occupations

The following table gives the percentages of total occupied population for the principal groups in the eight leading industrial countries prior to the World War.

Occupation	United States	Great Britain	France	Germany
Agriculture	35.64	12.66	41.42	35.11
Commercial occupations....	9.91	11.39	6.54	6.30
Conveyances of men, goods and messages	5.95	8.20	2.89	2.89
Mines and quarries........	2.09	5.00	1.59	3.25
Metals, machines, implements and conveyances..	3.72	7.89	4.35	6.99
Building and works of construction	4.43	6.77	4.20	6.99
Textile fabrics.............	2.02	6.92	4.55	3.75
Dress	4.29	7.23	8.05	5.39

	Austria	Hungary	Italy	Belgium
Agriculture	60.80	70.15	59.06	21.90
Commercial occupations....	3.34	2.56	3.43	11.79
Conveyance of men, goods and messages............	1.70	1.55	3.12	2.03
Mines and quarries........	1.56	.78	.89	6.46
Metals, machines, implements and conveyances..	2.78	2.15	2.14	5.95
Building and works of construction	2.96	1.48	5.02	7.28
Textile fabrics.............	3.26	.37	4.81	6.86
Dress	3.92	2.85	6.64	7.86

Influence of the Ocean on the Climate.—The ocean has much to do with the climate of its coast. As a rule, land on or near the ocean has more irregular weather, and is subject to more frequent changes than is territory some distance away from it. The ocean, besides, exercises a great influence on heat and cold. The land in close proximity to it has a warmer climate than territory far removed from it. While the thermometer in the summer may not show great variation, breezes coming from the ocean give an apparent coolness which does not exist inland. For this reason there are more summer resorts located on the ocean than away from it.

Insane.—There were in the United States in 1918 confined in insane asylums 239,820 persons, or 229.6 in every 100,000. In 1910 there were 187,791, or 204.2 in every 100,000.

Iron Industry.—The United States produces annually about 31,000,000 tons of pig iron and about 44,000,000 tons of steel.

Jewelry Industry.—Nearly $65,000,000 is invested in the manufacture of jewelry, and the annual value of the output exceeds $80,-000,000.

John Doe and Richard Roe.—Two fictitious names, used in law, one representing the plaintiff and the other the defendant. In writs of ejection these names are substituted when the real names of the parties are unknown or in doubt.

Kissing the Bible.—The Jews introduced the custom of swearing on the Bible, and the custom is still maintained throughout the civilized world, some of the courts even now requiring that the Bible be literally kissed before one gives testimony.

Koran.—The sacred book of the Mohammedans. The doctrine of the Koran is the unity of God and the existence of one true religion, with changeable ceremonies. Punishment for the bad, and rewards for the good, are presented and exemplified by stories taken from the Bible and other works. Most of the matter is supposed to have been borrowed from Jewish works, and bears traces of Jewish influence.

Language of Gems.—Amethyst represents peace of mind; Bloodstone signifies that one's absence is mourned; Diamond, pride; Emerald, success in love; Ruby stands for a cheerful mind; Sapphire represents chastity, and was supposed to stand for pure thoughts; Topaz, fidelity, and is supposed to calm the passions; Turquoise, happiness and success; Garnet, fidelity; Onyx, reciprocal love; Opal, pure thoughts; Pearl, innocence and purity.

Languages of the World.—It is estimated that there are 3424 distinct languages or dialects, about 1600 being spoken in America, about 940 in Asia, not far from 600 in Europe, and about 275 in Africa. Probably more than 150,000,000 people speak the English language, 120,000,000 the German, 90,000,000 Russian, 60,000,000 French, 55,000,000 Spanish, 40,-000,000 Italian, 30,000,000 Portuguese. The English language contain approximately 700,-000 words, about half of which are more or less technical and obsolete. Ordinary conversation does not require the use of more than 2,000 words. It is said that one can make himself understood in any language if his vocabulary is about 1,500 words.

Large Cities of North America

Akron, O	208,435	Bellingham, Wash...	25,585
Alameda, Cal	28,806	Beloit, Wis	21,284
Albany, N. Y	113,344	Berkeley, Cal	56,036
Allentown, Pa	73,502	Bethlehem, Pa	50,358
Alton, Ill	24,682	Beverly, Mass	22,561
Alliance, O	21,603	Binghamton, N. Y..	66,800
Altoona, Pa	60,331	Birmingham, Ala	178,806
Amsterdam, N. Y	33,524	Bloomfield, N. J	22,019
Anderson, Ind	29,767	Bloomington, Ill	28,725
Asheville, N. C	28,504	Boise, Ida	21,393
Ashtabula, O	22,082	Boston, Mass	748,060
Atlanta, Ga	200,616	Bridgeport, Conn	143,555
Atlantic City, N. J..	50,707	Brockton, Mass	66,254
Auburn, N. Y	36,192	Buffalo, N. Y	506,775
Augusta, Ga	52,548	Burlington, Ia	24,057
Aurora, Ill	36,397	Burlington, Vt	22,779
Austin, Tex	34,876	Butler, Pa	23,778
Baltimore, Md	733,826	Butte, Mont	41,611
Bangor, Me	25,978	Cambridge, Mass	109,694
Baton Rouge, La	21,782	Camden, N. J	116,309
Battle Creek, Mich..	36,164	Canton, O	87,091
Bay City, Mich	47,554	Cedar Rapids, Ia	45,566
Bayonne, N. J	76,754	Central Falls, R. I...	24,174
Beaumont, Tex	40,422	Charleston, S. C	67,957
Belleville, Ill	24,823	Charleston, W. Va..	39,608

Charlotte, N. C......	46,338	Flint, Mich.........	91,599
Chattanooga, Tenn...	57,895	Fond du Lac, Wis...	23,427
Chelsea, Mass.......	43,184	Fort Smith, Ark....	28,870
Chester, Pa.........	58,030	Fort Wayne, Ind....	86,549
Chicago, Ill........	2,701,705	Fort Worth, Tex...	106,482
Chicopee, Mass......	36,214	Fresno, Cal........	45,086
Cicero, Ill.........	44,995	Galesburg, Ill......	23,834
Cincinnati, O......	401,247	Galveston, Tex.....	44,255
Clarksburg, W. Va..	27,869	Gary, Ind..........	55,378
Cleveland, O.......	796,841	Gloucester, Mass....	22,947
Clifton, N. J.......	26,470	Gloversville, N. Y..	22,075
Clinton, Ia.........	24,151	Grand Rapids, Mich	137,634
Cohoes, N. Y.......	22,987	Great Falls, Mont..	24,121
Colorado Sp., Col....	30,105	Green Bay, Wis....	31,017
Columbia, S. C....	37,524	Greenville, S. C....	23,127
Columbus, Ga.......	31,125	Hagerstown, Md....	28,064
Columbus, O.......	237,031	Hamilton, O........	39,675
Concord, N. H......	22,167	Hammond, Ind......	36,004
Council Bluffs, Ia...	36,162	Harrisburg, Pa......	75,917
Covington, Ky......	57,121	Hartford, Conn.....	138,036
Cranston, R. I.....	29,407	Haverhill, Mass.....	53,884
Cumberland, Md....	29,837	Hazelton, Pa.......	32,277
Dallas, Tex.........	158,976	Hoboken, N. J......	68,166
Danville, Ill........	33,776	Holyoke, Mass......	60,203
Danville, Va........	21,539	Houston, Tex.......	138,276
Davenport, Ia.......	56,727	Huntington, W. Va..	50,177
Dayton, O.........	152,559	Hutchison, Kan.....	23,298
Decatur, Ill........	43,818	Indianapolis, Ind...	314,194
Denver, Col.......	256,491	Irvington, N. J.....	25,480
Des Moines, Ia......	126,468	Jackson, Mich.....	48,374
Detroit, Mich.......	993,678	Jackson, Miss.......	22,817
Dubuque, Ia.......	39,141	Jacksonville, Fla....	91,558
Duluth, Minn.......	98,917	Jamestown, N. Y...	38,917
Durham, N. C......	21,719	Jersey City, N. J..	298,103
East Liverpool, O...	21,411	Johnstown, Pa......	67,327
Easton, Pa..........	33,813	Joliet, Ill..........	38,442
East Orange, N. J..	50,710	Joplin, Mo.........	
East St. Louis, Ill..	66,767	Kalamazoo, Mich....	48,487
Eau Claire, Wis....	20,906	Kansas City, Kan...	101,177
Elgin, Ill..........	27,454	Kansas City, Mo....	324,410
Elizabeth, N. J.....	95,783	Kearney, N. Y....	26,724
Elkhart, Ind........	24,277	Kenosha, Wis.......	40,472
Elmira, N. Y.......	45,393	Kingston, N. Y....	26,688
El Paso, Tex......	77,560	Knoxville, Tenn.....	77,818
Elyria, O..........	20,474	Kokomo, Ind........	30,067
Erie, Pa...........	93,372	La Crosse, Wis.....	30,421
Evanston, Ill.......	37,234	Lafayette, Ind......	22,486
Evansville, Ind......	85,264	Lakewood, O.......	41,732
Everett, Mass......	40,120	Lancaster, Pa......	53,150
Everett, Wash......	27,644	Lansing, Mich......	57,327
Fall River, Mass...	120,485	Larado, Tex........	22,710
Fargo, N. Dak.....	21,961	Lawrence, Mass.....	94,270
Fitchburg, Mass.....	41,029	Lebanon, Pa........	24,643

Lewiston, Me	31,791	Newport News, Va	35,596
Lexington, Ky	41,534	New Rochelle, N. Y	36,213
Lima, O	41,326	Newton, Mass	46,054
Lincoln, Neb	54,948	New York, N. Y	5,620,048
Little Rock, Ark	65,142	Niagara Falls, N. Y	50,760
Lockport, N. Y	21,308	Norfolk, Va	115,777
Logansport, Ind	21,626	Norristown, Pa	32,319
Long Beach, Cal	55,593	North Adams, Mass	22,282
Lorain, O	37,295	Northampton, Mass	21,951
Los Angeles, Cal	576,673	Norwalk, Conn	27,743
Louisville, Ky	234,891	Norwich, Conn	22,304
Lowell, Mass	112,759	Norwood, O	24,966
Lynchburg, Va	30,070	Oakland, Cal	216,261
Lynn, Mass	99,148	Ogden, Utah	32,804
McKeesport, Pa	46,781	Oil City, Pa	21,274
Macon, Ga	52,995	Oklahoma, Okla	91,295
Macon City, Ia	20,065	Olean, N. Y	20,506
Madison, Wis	38,378	Omaha, Neb	191,601
Malden, Mass	49,103	Orange, N. J	33,268
Manchester, N. H	78,384	Oshkosh, Wis	33,162
Mansfield, O	27,824	Oswego, N. Y	23,626
Marion, Ind	23,747	Ottumwa, Ia	23,003
Marion, O	27,891	Paducah, Ky	24,735
Medford, Mass	39,038	Parkersburg, W. Va	20,050
Memphis, Tenn	162,351	Pasadena, Cal	45,354
Meriden, Conn	29,867	Passaic, N. J	63,841
Meridian, Miss	23,399	Paterson, N. J	135,875
Middletown, O	23,594	Pawtucket, R. I	64,248
Milwaukee, Wis	457,147	Pensacola, Fla	31,035
Minneapolis, Minn	380,582	Peoria, Ill	76,121
Mobile, Ala	60,777	Perth Amboy, N. J	41,707
Moline, Ill	30,734	Petersburg, Va	31,012
Montclair, N. J	28,810	Philadelphia, Pa	1,823,779
Montgomery, Ala	43,464	Phoenix, Ariz	29,053
Mt. Vernon, N. Y	42,726	Pittsburgh, Pa	588,343
Muncie, Ind	36,524	Pittsfield, Mass	41,763
Muskegon, Mich	36,570	Plainfield, N. J	27,700
Muskogee, Okla	30,277	Pontiac, Mich	34,273
Nashua, N. H	28,379	Port Arthur, Tex	22,251
Nashville, Tenn	118,342	Port Huron, Mich	25,944
New Albany, Ind	22,992	Portland, Me	69,272
Newark, N. J	414,524	Portland, Ore	258,288
Newark, O	26,718	Portsmouth, O	33,011
New Bedford, Mass	121,217	Portsmouth, Va	54,387
New Britain, Conn	59,316	Pottsville, Pa	21,876
New Brunswick, N. J	32,779	Poughkeepsie, N. Y	35,000
Newburgh, N. Y	30,366	Providence, R. I	237,595
New Castle, Pa	44,938	Pueblo, Col	43,050
New Haven, Conn	162,537	Quincy, Ill	35,978
New London, Conn	25,688	Quincy, Mass	47,876
New Orleans, La	387,219	Racine, Wis	58,593
Newport, Ky	29,317	Raleigh, N. C	24,418
Newport, R. I	30,255	Reading, Pa	107,784

Revere, Mass.......	28,823	Terre Haute, Ind....	66,083
Richmond, Ind......	26,765	Toledo, O..........	243,164
Richmond, Va......	171,667	Topeka, Kan.......	50,022
Roanoke, Va........	50,842	Trenton, N. J......	119,289
Rochester, N. Y....	295,750	Troy, N. Y........	72,013
Rockford, Ill.......	65,651	Tucson, Ariz........	20,292
Rock Island, Ill....	35,177	Tulsa, Okla........	72,075
Rome, N. Y.......	26,341	Union, N. J........	20,651
Sacramento, Cal....	65,908	Utica, N. Y.......	94,156
Saginaw, Mich......	61,903	Vallejo, Cal.........	21,107
St. Joseph, Mo......	77,939	Waco, Tex.........	38,500
St. Louis, Mo......	772,897	Waltham, Mass.....	30,915
St. Paul, Minn.....	234,698	Warren, O.........	27,050
Salem, Mass........	42,529	Waterbury, Conn....	91,715
Salt Lake City, Utah	118,110	Waterloo, Ia........	36,230
San Antonio, Tex..	161,379	Watertown, N. Y...	31,285
San Diego, Cal.....	74,683	Wheeling, W. Va....	56,208
Sandusky, O........	22,897	White Plains, N. Y..	21,031
San Francisco, Cal.	506,676	Wichita, Kan.......	72,217
San Jose, Cal.....	39,642	Wichita Falls, Tex..	40,079
Savannah, Ga.......	83,252	Wilkes Barre, Pa...	73,833
Schenectady, N. Y..	88,723	Williamsport, Pa....	36,198
Scranton, Pa.......	137,783	Wilmington, Del....	110,168
Seattle, Wash......	315,312	Wilmington, N. C...	33,372
Sedalia, Mo.........	21,144	Winston-Salem, N. C	48,395
Sharon, Pa.........	21,747	Woonsocket, R. I...	43,496
Sheboygan, Wis.....	30,955	Worcester, Mass....	179,754
Shenandoah, Pa.....	24,726	Yonkers, N. Y.....	100,176
Shreveport, La......	43,874	York, Pa...........	47,512
Sioux City, Ia......	71,227	Youngstown, O.....	132,358
Sioux Falls, S. Dak	25,202	Zanesville, O.......	29,569
Somerville, Mass....	93,091		
South Bend, Ind....	70,893	Calgary, Alberta....	43,704
Spartanburg, S. C...	22,638	Edmonton, Alberta..	24,900
Spokane, Wash.....	104,437	Halifax, N. S......	46,619
Springfield, Ill......	59,183	Hamilton, Ont......	81,169
Springfield, Mass...	129,614	London, Ont........	46,300
Springfield, Mo.....	39,631	Montreal, Que......	800,000
Springfield, O.......	60,840	Ottawa, Ont........	112,232
Stamford, Conn....	35,096	Quebec, Que.......	78,190
Steubenville, O......	28,508	Regina, Sask.......	30,213
Stockton, Cal.......	40,296	St. John, N. B.....	42,511
Superior, Wis......	39,671	Toronto, Ont........	376,538
Syracuse, N. Y....	171,717	Vancouver, B. C...	195,000
Tacoma, Wash	96,965	Victoria, B. C......	31,660
Tampa, Fla.........	51,608	Winnipeg, Man.....	136,035
Taunton, Mass......	37,137		

Large Cities of the World

(Exclusive of the United States and Canada)

Adelaide, Australia..	225,000	Duisburg, Germany.	230,000
Armedabad, India...	216,800	Dusseldorf, Germany	360,000
Aleppo, Syria.......	250,000	Edinburgh, Scotland.	333,883
Alexandria, Egypt..	444,600	Ekaterinoslav, Russia	200,000
Algiers, Algeria....	200,000	Essen, Germany.....	460,000
Amsterdam, Holland	650,000	Florence, Italy......	250,000
Bagdad, Mesopotamia	200,000	Foochow, China.....	650,000
Bahia, Brazil.......	400,000	Frankfort, Germany.	415,000
Baku, Russia.......	240,000	Genoa, Italy........	325,000
Bangkok, Siam......	541,000	Glasgow, Scotland...1,111,428	
Barcelona, Spain....	625,000	Goteborg, Sweden...	200,000
Batavia, Java.......	240,000	The Hague, Holland	360,000
Balem, Brazil.......	300,000	Halle, Germany.....	200,000
Belfast, Ireland.....	393,000	Hamburg, Germany..1,000,000	
Benares, India......	204,000	Hangchow, China....	700,000
Berlin, Germany....1,900,000		Hankow, China.....1,500,000	
Birmingham, England	861,585	Hanover, China.....1,500,000	
Bologna, Italy......	200,000	Havana, Cuba........	361,000
Bombay, India......	979,000	Havre, France......	200,000
Bordeaux, France...	400,000	Helsingfors, Finland	200,000
Bradford, England...	282,714	Hong Kong, China..	561,000
Bremen, Germany...	300,000	Hyderabad, India....	500,600
Breslau, Germany...	520,000	Kazan, Russia......	200,000
Bristol, England.....	361,247	Kharkov, Russia....	250,000
Brno, Czech-Slovakia	225,000	Kiel, Germany......	220,000
Brussels, Belgium...	680,000	Kiev, Russia........600,000	
Bucharest, Roumania	350,000	Kingston, England..	279,664
Budapest, Hungary.	900,000	Kobe, Japan........	510,000
Buenos Aires, Argen	1,637,000	Konigsberg, Germany	250,000
Cairo, Egypt........	791,000	Kyoto, Japan.......	550,000
Calcutta, India......1,222,000		Lahore, India.......	228,700
Canton, China......	950,000	Leeds, England.....	430,834
Catania, Italy.......	225,000	Leicester, England..	236,059
Changsha, China....	550,000	Leipsig, Germany...	600,000
Charlottenburg, Ger.	310,000	Lille, France.......	375,000
Chemnitz, Germany.	290,000	Lisbon, Portugal....	450,000
Chalon, Fr Ind China	200,000	Liverpool, England..	772,665
Christiania, Norway.	260,000	Lodz, Poland.......	430,000
Chungking, China...	440,000	London, Greater, Eng	7,258,263
Cologne, Germany...	525,000	Lucknow, India.....	259,800
Constantinople, Turk	1,000,000	Lwow, Poland......	210,000
Copenhagen, Denmark	650,000	Lyon, France.......	700,000
Damascus, Syria....	250,000	Madras, India......	518,600
Danzig, Baltic......	200,000	Madrid, Spain......	655,000
Delhi, India........	233,000	Magdeburg, Germany	280,000
Dortmund, Germany	250,000	Manchester, England	741,068
Dresden, Germany..	550,000	Mannheim, Germany	200,000
Dublin, Ireland.....	399,000	Marseilles, France...	800,000

Melbourne, Australia	723,500	Rotterdam, Holland..	510,000
Mexico City, Mexico	1,000,000	Santiago, Chile......	430,000
Milan, Italy........	690,000	Sao Paulo, Brazil..	510,000
Montevideo, Uruguay	362,000	Saratov, Russia.....	230,000
Moscow, Russia....	1,100,000	Seoul, Korea.......	310,000
Munich, Germany...	600,000	Shanghai, China....	1,100,000
Nagoya, Japan......	400,000	Sheffield, England...	473,695
Nanking, China.....	390,000	Singapore, Straits Set	846,000
Nantes, France......	220,000	Soochow, China......	550,000
Naples, Italy........	700,000	Stettin, Germany....	230,000
Neu Kolln, Germany	250,000	Stockholm, Sweden..	410,000
Newcastle, England..	275,099	Strassbourg, France.	225,000
Nice, France........	200,000	Stuttgart, Germany..	290,000
Ningpo, China......	700,000	Sydney, Australia...	792,700
Nottingham, England	275,573	Tabriz, Persia......	200,000
Nurnberg, Germany..	335,000	Tashkent, Siberia...	275,000
Odessa, Russia......	600,000	Teheran, Persia.....	225,000
Oporto, Portugal....	200,000	Tientsin, China.....	800,000
Osaka, Japan.......	1,500,000	Tiflis, Georgian Repub	346,000
Palermo, Italy......	360,000	Tokio, Japan........	2,400,000
Paris, France......	3,300,000	Toronto, Canada....	562,585
Pekin, China.......	1,200,000	Tunis, Africa.......	200,000
Pernambuco, Brazil..	250,000	Turin, Italy........	460,000
Petrograd, Russia...	2,300,000	Valencia, Spain.....	250,000
Portsmouth, England	224,846	Valparaiso, Chile....	230,000
Prague, Bohemia....	700,000	Venice, Italy.......	200,000
Rangoon, India.....	293,300	Vienna, Austria.....	2,400,000
Riga, Latvia........	570,000	Vilna, Lithuania....	215,000
Riga, Russia........	550,000	Warsaw, Poland....	825,000
Rio de Janeiro, Bra	1,200,000	Wenchow, China.....	225,000
Rome, Italy.........	600,000	Winnipeg, Canada...	136,035
Rosario, Argentia...	222,600	Yokohama, Japan....	450,000
Rostov, Russia.....	200,000	Zurich, Switzerland..	213,000

Law—Every one within the United States is amenable: first, to the laws laid down by the Constitution of the United States; secondly, to any laws which may be made by Congress; thirdly, to State laws; fourthly, to county law; fifthly, to local ordinances passed by the city or town. No local ordinance can be forced if it is contrary to the law of the State, and no State law holds if it is at variance with the Constitution of the United States. The Supreme Court of each State passes upon the constitutionality of all laws made within the State, and the Supreme Court of the United States is the final Court of appeal. A law made by Congress is not valid if it is declared unconstitutional by the Supreme Court of the United States, nor may any State law be enforced if the Supreme Court of that State considers it unconstitutional.

Literature.—Literature is not, and probably never will be, satisfactorily defined. Broadly speaking, it is any form of written or printed words upon any subject. More specifically defined, the term "literature" would apply to essays, poetry, stories, and other works of fiction of the grade acceptable to the best magazines and book publishers. Works of history may be called literature, and scientific works come under this classification; but historical writers are usually called historians, and scientific writers are known as scientists. Story writers are usually classified as novelists, and newspaper writers as journalists. A book, commonly, if not technically, speaking, is a volume usually bound in board covers and containing one hundred or more pages, but it may be a book if there are only a dozen pages with covers of paper.

Magnetic Poles.—The magnetic poles are not, as most people suppose, identical with the geographical poles, the north magnetic pole being south of the geographical North Pole, and the south magnetic pole being north of the geographical South Pole. The north magnetic pole is located at about 77° 59′, and the south at about 72° 23′.

Mammoth Cave.—Mammoth Cave, probably the best known of similar freaks of Nature, is located in Kentucky, and has a length of nine miles. It contains many avenues, chambers, domes, lakes, rivers, and waterfalls. Echo River, inside of the cave, is ¾ of a mile in length, from a few feet to 200 ft. wide, and has a depth of from 10 to 30 ft. It is well filled with fish, none of which have eyes.

Meat Industry.—There are, in the United States, about 1650 slaughter houses employing nearly 110,000 people with about $4,000,000 capital invested. The annual product of the meat industry is not far from $1,400,000,000.

Medicine Chests.—Every one should maintain a medicine chest or shelf containing simple remedies, but these should never be selected without the advice of a physician. Thousands of persons injure themselves by self-dosing. When in the slightest doubt, visit or call your doctor. Most ailments can be prevented or cured by a skillful physician, but if allowed to run they may result seriously or fatally. Do not take chances with yourself.

Microscope.—The first microscope is said to have been invented by a Dutchman in 1590, but its invention has been attributed to Galileo in 1610. The microscope has been perfected until a millionth part of a grain of blood may be detected by means of the spectrum lens.

Mineral Industry... The minerals mined in the United States every year have a value of about $4,653,700,000.

Mining Industry.—Nearly 1,140,000 men are engaged in the mines of the United States, over 90 per cent of whom are wage earners.

Moon.—The moon is the earth's only satellite. It circles around the earth every 27 days, 7 hours, and 43.2 minutes, on the average; but because its motion is common with the earth around the sun, the mean duration of the lunar month is 29 days, 12 hours, 44.05 minutes. The distance from the earth to the moon is from 238,850 to 252,820 miles, although at times the moon is only 216,477 miles from the earth. The moon's diameter is 2,162 miles. The surface of the moon contains about 14,685,000 square miles, or about four times the area of Europe. The moon, although very much smaller than the planets, exerts a stronger attractive force on the earth because of its nearness. The moon is, unscientifically speaking, drawing everything on the earth towards it, while at the same time the earth is exerting the same attractive force upon the moon. Because of this, the oceans, being composed of water, which is easily movable, respond and move with the moon, causing the tides. This same attractive force is brought to bear upon the earth itself, but because it is of greater density it is not perceptibly affected. Theoretically, every lake and pond has a tide, but the motion of the water is too slight to be measured. The moon is supposed to possess neither atmosphere nor water. Thousands of ages ago the lunar surface was subjected to terrible volcanic actions which forced the land into ridges, some of them supposed to exceed 20,000 feet in height, and rents and depressions of corresponding depths. The surface of the moon appears to be desolate and to be unfitted to support any form of life.

Mortality.—About 12.9 people out of every thousand of the population of the United States die during each year. The percentage

of male deaths is somewhat larger than that
of female, due to accidents. The annual death
rate per thousand is: 13.6 in Los Angeles, 15.9
in San Francisco, 14.7 in Denver, 14.7 in Washington, D. C., 12.5 in Chicago, 13.4 in Indian-
apolis, 17.3 in Louisville, 18.9 in New Orleans,
15.7 in Baltimore, 15.7 in Boston, 14.0 in Detroit, 11.7 in Minneapolis, 11.9 in St. Paul,
15.3 in Kansas City, 13.3 in St. Louis, 12.8 in
Omaha, 13.3 in New York, 15.9 in Cincinnati,
12.6 in Cleveland, 14.3 in Philadelphia, 16.1
in Pittsburgh, 21.4 in Memphis.

Mortgages.—A mortgage is a bill-of-sale
from the owner of property to another competent to hold property. The one giving the
mortgage is called the mortgagee, and the one
to whom it is made is known as the mortgagor. A mortgage differs from a bill-of-sale
in that the mortgagor cannot obtain ownership of the property mortgaged, unless the
amount involved is not paid him at the expiration of the mortgage, or the interest is not
met. All mortgages must be registered.
Mortgaged property cannot be moved, altered,
or changed without the consent of the mortgagor. The property, unless it is land, should
be insured, and the insurance policy made
payable to the mortgagor in case of loss by
fire, but the mortgagor can collect only that
part of the insurance money which represents
the amount of the mortgage. Should the
mortgagee fail to pay interest at the period

stated in the mortgage, or should he be unable or refuse to liquidate the mortgage at its expiration, the mortgagor cannot seize the property except by act of law. It must be advertised and sold at auction. If the mortgaged property brings a price lower than the face of the mortgage, the mortgagor loses the difference, and has to bear the expense of foreclosure. If more than the face of the mortgage is realized, the mortgagee is entitled to what is received, less the face of the mortgage and the expenses of foreclosure.

Natural Gas.—A gas generated underground, and due to chemical action beneath the earth's surface. It is found in various parts of the world, and is used for fuel and illuminating, largely for the former.

Naturalization.—Any foreigner or alien, except those of the Mongolian or Brown Race, may become a citizen of the United States, and be entitled to every privilege granted to natural-born citizens, except that he cannot become President or Vice-President of the United States. An alien cannot make application for naturalization or citizenship until he is 18 years of age, and he cannot apply for his Second or Final Paper of Naturalization until he has lived in the United States for at least five years, and he must make his Declaration of Intention two or more years before he applies for his Second or Final

Paper. The applicant must be a resident of the State in which he makes petition for naturalization not less than one year, and have lived at least four years additional in the same State, or in some other State. He must make application to the United States District Court in the State in which he lives. The cost of becoming naturalized is less than $5.00. A married woman does not have to be naturalized if her husband has become a citizen of the United States, and the children of the naturalized parents become citizens at 21 years of age without taking out naturalization papers. Full particulars regarding the process of naturalization are very plainly and explicitly stated in a book entitled " How to Obtain Citizenship," by Nathaniel C. Fowler, Jr.

Newspapers.—A newspaper is a periodical issued as often as once a week, and contains the news of the day, either local or general, or both. The majority of newspapers are of four or eight pages, but often the number of pages run as high as 24, or even 72, and occasionally 100 pages are issued at a time. In the United States and Canada, there are published over 2,600 daily newspapers, about 75 tri-weekly, a little less than 650 semi-weekly, considerable more than 17,000 weekly. Of other periodicals, about 60 are published every two weeks, somewhat less than 300 semi-monthly, more than 3,000 monthly, about 80 bi-monthly, and less than 250 quarterly. Periodicals published less often than once a week are not considered newspapers, although they may contain news. There are over 60,000 newspapers published in the world.

New York Stock Exchange.—A single seat, carrying with it membership in the New York Stock Exchange, has been sold for as much as $110,000.

Nicknames of States.—Alabama, " Cotton State "; Alaska, " Eldorado of the North "; Arkansas, " Bear "; California, " Golden Land "; Colorado, " Centennial State "; Connecticut, " Nutmeg "; Delaware, " Blue Hen " and " Diamond State "; Florida, " Gulf " and " Flowery State "; Georgia, " Cracker State "; Indiana, " Hoosier State "; Iowa, " Hawkeye "; Kansas, " Prairie "; Kentucky, " Blue Grass State "; Louisiana, " Creole State "; Maine, " Pine Tree State "; Maryland, " Old Line State "; Massachusetts, " Old Bay State "; Michigan, " Lake State "; Minnesota, " Gopher State "; Mississippi, " Bayou State "; Missouri, " Bullion State "; Montana, " Mountain State "; Nebraska, " Black Water State "; Nevada, " Silver State "; New Hampshire, " Granite State "; New Jersey, " Red Mud State "; New York, " Empire State "; North Carolina, " Old North State "; North Dakota, " Cyclone State "; Ohio, " Buckeye State "; Oklahoma, " Boomer State "; Oregon, " Bea-

ver State "; Pennsylvania, " Keystone State ";
Rhode Island, " Little Rhody "; Tennessee,
" Old Franklin State "; South Carolina, " Pal-
metto State "; South Dakota, " Blizzard
State "; Texas, " Lone-Star State "; Utah,
" Mormon State "; Vermont, " Green Moun-
tain State "; Virginia, " Old Dominion ";
West Virginia, " Panhandle State "; Wiscon-
sin, " Badger State ".

Nitroglycerine.—Nitroglycerine is made of
common glycerine mixed with strong nitric
and sulphuric acids, and is extremely explosive
and dangerous. It has to be exploded by concussion or shock, and not by fire. It is used
for blasting and other purposes, and occas-
sionally is taken in very small doses as a medicine, but never should be used medicinally except by the advice of a physician who should
be present when it is taken.

Notes.—A note should be signed in ink, but
a pencil signature is good in law. A note is
not payable on demand unless it so states. A
note may be payable to order or to bearer. If
payable to order, and transferred, it must be
endorsed. The endorser of a note is liable for
its payment, if the maker of it does not pay it.
Each signer of a joint note is liable for the
full amount. Notes do not bear interest unless so stated. " Value received " should be
written in every note, but it is not essential.

Ocean Ownership.—The ocean is common

property, and no one has any legal title to it, except that each country has jurisdiction over the sea within three miles of the shore, but these three miles are usually reckoned from promontories, and not necessarily from the coast-line, so that a nation may have control of a vast area of water and several hundred miles from shore.

Old Time Ships.—The glory of the American merchant service, so far as sailing vessels are concerned, has passed into history. Comparatively few sailing vessels, save coasting schooners, ply the seas, as steam has taken the place of sail. The majority of old ship captains are either dead or commanding ocean liners or coastwise steamers. In the old days, sailing clipper ships made the trip from New York to San Francisco in one hundred days, while the voyage of ordinary ships was two or three times as long. The old ship "Lightning" sailed from Boston to Liverpool at a greater speed than that obtained by any steamship of its day, the vessel often logging over 500 miles in 24 hours, and it made the trip in a little less than 14 days. The "James Baines" sailed from Boston to Liverpool in 12 days and 6 hours, and broke the sailing record between these two ports. The same vessel made the trip from Liverpool to Melbourne, Australia, in 63 days and returned in 69 days. The "Red Jacket" sailed from New

York to Liverpool in 13 days, 1 hour, and 25 minutes. The "Flying Cloud" and "Andrew Jackson" sailed from New York to San Francisco in 89 days, and the "Sea Witch" made the trip from Canton, China, to New York in 74 days, 14 hours. These early clipper ships were quite small, many of them not being over 200 tons. The first large clipper ship was the "Ann McKim," which was 43 ft. long, and 493 tons burden. Subsequent sailing vessels of enormous size were built, the "John Bertram" having a tonnage of 1080, the "Gamecock" 1,320, the "Staghound" 1,535, the "Flying Cloud" 1,783, the "Staffordshire" 1,817, the "Sovereign of the Seas" 2,421 tons, and the "Great Republic" 4,555 tons.

Palmistry.—The study of the lines of the palm, which the ancients believed indicated character and future. Palmistry is to-day practiced by three classes of people: (1) professional palmists, most of whom are charlatans; (2) as a diversion; (3) by superstitious people who believe in it. A scientific study of the subject does not furnish any evidence that the lines of the hand have any special significance, and no scientific person gives them any credence.

Partnership.—A partnership is an agreement, usually written, between two or more persons, for the doing of business or for the carrying out of any contract or for the accomplishment of any work. The partners may have equal ownership, or it may be unevenly divided. In the equal partnerships, each partner has the same financial interest and share in the profits, and also the same right of control. In other partnerships, the financial investment or interests are unevenly divided; and the one who holds more than half interest controls the business, unless otherwise provided for in the partnership agreement. Partners may be in name only, and not own any of the property. Active partners are those who give practically all of their time to the conducting of the business. Silent partners are not likely to take any active part in the management of the business, but they may control it, if their financial interest is sufficient. Under common law, no partner has a right to engage in any other business which would injure the partnership, unless permitted to do so by the other partners. The acts of one partner bind all of the rest. If one partner commits fraud in the name of the firm, the others are financially responsible, although they may have had no knowledge of his action. The partnership or business may or may not be liable for the private debts of any one partner. Usually a partner cannot be held for more than his interest in the firm. Partnerships may be dissolved by mutual agreement or by judicial act, and it is usual to publish the dissolution of partnership in one or more of the local newspapers, and to send notices of it to the trade. A limited partnership does not hold any partner or the concern itself liable for more than the amount of the property in the business, but a partnership will not be considered limited unless it is publicly announced.

Patent Medicines

It has been said, and with some degree of truth, that Americans are self-dosers, and that they are prone to attempt to cure themselves, even of serious diseases, without consulting a physician.

The sale of patent medicines is enormous, although I think it is diminishing in volume, due to the exposures which have appeared in many periodicals, and to the better education of the people.

A patent medicine, technically speaking, is a concoction or drug, or combination of drugs, claimed to be a remedy or cure for a specific ill or for all of the ills that the human flesh is heir to. It is manufactured in large quantities, and bottled or put up with attractive labels, with more or less directions given for its use. Many of the patent medicines are either absolutely ineffective or are positively dangerous. Many of them contain a large percentage of alcohol, which acts as a transient tonic, and produces an exhiliration which the sufferer is likely to consider beneficial.

The effect of the alcohol soon wears off, and the taker is much worse for having swallowed it.

Other patent medicines contain cocaine and other dangerous drugs, which never should be taken without the advice of a physician. The effect of some patent medicines is likely to be immediate and to appear to be efficacious. Some patent medicines, however, are made of pure drugs, and are really valuable. I am, however, opposed to the use of patent medicines, even of those which are carefully and scientifically compounded.

It is obvious that the layman cannot diagnose his trouble, and the label on the bottle, or the pamphlet accompanying it, is likely to confuse him, and in many cases makes him feel that he is suffering from an ailment or disease which does not exist.

Headache powders, cough medicines, tonics of all kinds, soothing syrup for babies, should be conscientiously avoided, unless prescribed by a physician. They are likely to contain dangerous drugs, and may have no medicinal properties at all.

Because a certain medicine has worked well with one person should not be taken as evidence that another can take it to his advantage. Similar symptoms may exist, and yet the root of the trouble be entirely different.

Even if every patent medicine were pure and scientifically compounded, I would advise against their use, unless recommended by a physician, who is likely to diagnose correctly the trouble and to apply the right remedy.

Physicians are not infallible, but every reputable physician is a graduate of a medical school, a reader of current medical magazines, and is constantly in touch, by experience, with other physicians and with human ailments. Even if he is not an expert, his close proximity to disease makes him far more reliable than the label on the medicine bottle.

I would advise no one to place himself in the hands of any physician who is not a member of one of the great medical associations, maintained by both the allopathic and homeopathic schools.

These associations will not admit into membership any one who has not been properly instructed, and who is not reliable. Any physician of standing, and with a sufficient knowledge of the human body, can obtain membership in these associations, and those who are not members may be looked upon with suspicion, although it is quite likely that some of them are reliable; but as they are outside of the associations, they cannot have the facilities of consultation and experience, which are given to those in regular standing in an association.

It is obvious that one of even ordinary ability, who is educated in the profession, is more reliable than one who doctors by his wits, even though he may appear to be successful. Although there are some charlatans in the profession, who practice in their own interest more than in that of their patients, the average physician represents the highest order of civilization. He knows at the start that his profession is not likely to bring him heavy financial return. He goes into it with his eyes open. He is under the strictest rules and regulations, and cannot maintain his standing in the associations, or with the public, if he does not practice legitimately. He has every facility at his command, and although he is not always successful, he is far better able to produce results than is one who has not been properly educated, and who lacks experience and association with other doctors, and who has not had hospital practice. Every reputable physician has not only graduated from a medical school, but was given opportunity to practice in hospitals and elsewhere before he became a family physician. The so-called specialist began as a family physician, and gives his time somewhat exclusively to one disease or to surgery. The surgeon, while a regular physician, specializes in surgery, and comparatively few family practitioners will handle a serious surgical case, except in emergencies. They refer the patient to the skilled surgeon.

The physician is both a curer and preventor of disease. I would advise every one, no matter how healthy he may be, to consult a reputable physician once a year, and to be overhauled, so to speak. Most troubles can be obviated if taken in time. A symptom seemingly serious to the one having it may be of little consequence, and yet it may be the forerunner of an incurable disease. If a good physician is consulted in time, he may either obviate the trouble or prevent its rapid increase. No one should attempt to diagnose his own condition. Even the physician will not do so for himself, because no one can tell by his feelings exactly what is the matter with him or what would better be done. The physician when sick, consults other physicians, if his trouble is of any seriousness. The expense of an annual examination need not exceed two or three dollars, and some physicians will make it for a dollar. They are likely to locate any trouble, although it may have just appeared and the symptom be slight. They will prescribe a treatment, which cannot fail to be of benefit to those who consult them. Therefore, I say, visit a good physician at least once a year, irrespective of your health.

In every city, and in many of the towns, are practicing alleged physicians or doctors, who claim to be unusually expert and able to cure where others fail, or even to cure what cannot be cured. Some of them are graduates of medical schools, and are really good physicians, but most of them are irresponsible and without real ability. Their method frequently makes the patient feel that he is being cured, and cured rapidly. They use appliances and drugs which have an immediate effect, usually to the patients' injury; or they practice the same as regular physicians do and give the patient false encouragement. It seems to me obvious that no so-called outside practitioner, who is not a member of the associations, can possibly possess any information or know of any method of treatment with which the regular physicians are unfamiliar. These charlatans play upon the feelings of the patient, and it is said that some of them keep him sick for financial reasons. Therefore, I warn the reader against any physician who is not a member of one of the two great associations, and who is not recognized by the profession at large. Even though some of them are skillful, it is safer to employ a physician of standing than to take one who makes a business of practicing, and who is not answerable to the rules and regulations enforced by the associations, and who cannot, because of his removal from them, obtain and enjoy the privilege of consultation with other members of his craft. Do not take chances with your body. Better risk the few mistakes made by physicians than by your own doctor.

Perpetual Motion.—Scientists, particularly early ones, made frantic and continuous en' deavors to invent what was supposed to be perpetual motion; that is, a machine which will keep perpetually in motion without being replenished or supplied with outside energy. About 60 years ago scientific bodies refused to consider it, as it was proved to be impossible. The " Scientific American," many years ago, likened perpetual motion to an energy which will permit a man to lift himself by his boot-straps.

Petroleum Industry.—The annual production is considerably more than 15,000,000,000 gallons a year.

Philippine Islands.—The Philippine Islands consist of 7,083 islands, having an area of about 115,000 square miles. The population is 10,350,640. It has a coast line of 11,444 statute miles, which exceeds that of the entire United States. The climate is tropical.

Pianoforte.—The piano or pianoforte is said to have been invented in Italy and to have appeared in 1714. Germany, however, claims the honor of its invention. It was introduced into England in 1766.

Plate Glass.—The sand, out of which glass is made, is melted until it is of about the consistency of molasses. It is then poured into a casting trough or a table mounted on wheels so it can be run close to the mouth of the furnace. The molten glass is poured into the trough through a sluice-way, and before it hardens, heavy rollers pass over it, reducing it to the required thickness. It is rolled to about 9-16 of an inch, and then by further rolling and polishing it is reduced to the required thickness. It further passes through a smelting oven which thoroughly hardens it. Then, it is again polished.

Playing Cards.—The origin is unknown, although they appeared in Europe in 1350. It is claimed that the Arabs used playing cards at a much earlier date. It is estimated that over sixteen million packs of playing cards are made annually in the United States.

Pole Star.—This is a star of the second magnitude, found at the extremity of the handle of the Little Dipper.

Population and Land Area of the United States

Geographic Division and State	Population, 1920	Land area (square miles), 1920
CONTINENTAL UNITED STATES	105,710,620	2,973,774
GEOGRAPHIC DIVISIONS:		
New England	7,400,909	61,976
Middle Atlantic	22,261,144	100,000
East North Central	21,475,543	245,564
West North Central	12,544,249	510,804
South Atlantic	13,990,272	269,071
East South Central	8,893,307	179,509

West South Central	10,242,224	429,746
Mountain	3,336,101	859,009
Pacific	5,566,871	318,095
NEW ENGLAND:		
Maine	768,014	29,895
New Hampshire	443,083	9,031
Vermont	352,428	9,124
Massachusetts	3,852,356	8,039
Rhode Island	604,397	1,067
Connecticut	1,380,631	4,820
MIDDLE ATLANTIC:		
New York	10,385,227	47,654
New Jersey	3,155,900	7,514
Pennsylvania	8,720,017	44,832
EAST NORTH CENTRAL:		
Ohio	5,759,394	40,740
Indiana	2,930,390	36,045
Illinois	6,485,280	56,043
Michigan	3,668,412	57,480
Wisconsin	2,632,067	55,256
WEST NORTH CENTRAL:		
Minnesota	2,387,125	80,858
Iowa	2,404,021	55,586
Missouri	3,404,055	68,727
North Dakota	646,872	70,183
South Dakota	636,547	76,868
Nebraska	1,296,372	76,808
Kansas	1,769,257	81,774
SOUTH ATLANTIC:		
Delaware	223,003	1,965
Maryland	1,449,661	9,941
District of Columbia	437,571	60
Virginia	2,309,187	40,262
West Virginia	1,463,701	24,022
North Carolina	2,559,123	48,740
South Carolina	1,683,724	30,495
Georgia	2,895,832	58,725
Florida	968,470	54,861
EAST SOUTH CENTRAL:		
Kentucky	2,416,630	40,181
Tennessee	2,337,885	41,687

Alabama	2,348,174	51,279
Mississippi	1,790,618	46,362
WEST SOUTH CENTRAL:		
Arkansas	1,752,204	52,525
Louisiana	1,798,509	45,409
Oklahoma	2,028,283	69,414
Texas	4,663,228	262,398
MOUNTAIN:		
Montana	548,889	146,131
Idaho	431,866	83,354
Wyoming	194,402	97,548
Colorado	939,629	103,658
New Mexico	360,350	122,503
Arizona	334,162	113,810
Utah	449,396	82,184
Nevada	77,407	109,821
PACIFIC:		
Washington	1,356,621	66,836
Oregon	783,389	95,607
California	3,426,861	155,652

Population Per Square Mile

Continental United States.—The following summary shows, for continental United States, the total population, land area in square miles, and population per square mile of land area at each census from 1790 to 1920, inclusive:

Census Year	Population	Land area (square miles)	Population per sq. mile
1920	105,710,620	2,973,774	35.5
1910	91,972,266	2,973,890	30.9
1900	75,994,575	2,974,159	25.6
1890	62,947,714	2,973,965	21.2

1880	50,155,783	2,973,965	16.9
1870	38,558,371	2,973,965	13.0
1860	31,443,321	2,973,965	10.6
1850	23,191,876	2,944,337	7.9
1840	17,069,453	1,753,588	9.7
1830	12,866,020	1,753,588	7.3
1820	9,638,453	1,753,588	55.
1810	7,239,881	1,685,865	4.3
1800	5,308,483	867,980	6.1
1790	3,929,214	867,980	4.5

According to the census of 1920, there are in continental United States, on the average, 35.5 inhabitants to each square mile of land area, or almost eight times the number per square mile shown for the much smaller area of 1790, and over three and a half times the number for 1860. The decrease in the average number of inhabitants per square mile at the census of 1810 and 1850 was due in each case to large accessions of thinly populated territory during the decade preceding the census.

In the order of their density of population the nine geographic divisions of the country rank as follows: Middle Atlantic, 222.6 inhabitants per square mile; New England, 119.4; East North Central, 87.5 South Atlantic, 52.0; East South Central, 49.5; West North Central, 24.6; West South Central, 23.8; Pacific, 17.5; and Mountain, 3.9 The changes in density from census to census correspond precisely with the changes in area and the total number of inhabitants. It may be noted, however, that on account of the rapid increase in their population the Pacific states in 1910 for the first time are approaching, in density of population, conditions found in the states between the Mississippi River and the Rocky Mountains.

Porto Rico.—Porto Rico contains over 3,400 square miles, and has a population of more than 1,200,000. The climate is tropical and the land is extremely fertile.

Postage Stamps.—They were invented in 1834, and were introduced into America in 1847.

Poultry and Egg Industry.—Nearly 500,000-000 of poultry, including chickens, turkeys, geese, and pigeons, are raised in the United States annually. The total value is about $203,000,000. Each year the production of eggs is about 1,600,000,000 dozen. The people of the United States eat about 5½ fowls per year per capita, and a little over 17 dozen eggs.

Presidents of the United States

(1) George Washington.
(2) John Adams.
(3) Thomas Jefferson.
(4) James Madison.
(5) James Monroe.
(6) John Quincy Adams.
(7) Andrew Jackson.

(8) Martin Van Buren.
(9) William Henry Harrison.
(10) John Tyler.
(11) James K. Polk.
(12) Zachary Taylor.
(13) Millard Fillmore.
(14) Franklin Pierce.
(15) James Buchanan.
(16) Abraham Lincoln.
(17) Andrew Johnson.
(18) Ulysses S. Grant.
(19) Rutherford B. Hayes.
(20) James A. Garfield.
(21) Chester A. Arthur.
(22) Grover Cleveland.
(23) Benjamin Harrison.
(24) William McKinley.
(25) Theodore Roosevelt.
(26) William H. Taft.
(27) Woodrow Wilson.
(28) Warren G. Harding.

Principal Countries of the World

COUNTRY	CAPITAL	SQ. MILES	POPULATION
Abyssinia	Addis Abeba	350,000	8,000,000
Afghanistan	Kabul	245,000	6,380,500
Argentina	Buenos Aires	1,131,841	8,300,000
Australia	Melbourne	3,063,041	5,000,000
Austria	Vienna	31,000	6,500,000
Belgium	Brussels	11,400	7,500,000
Bolivia	Sucre	570,000	3,000,000
Brazil	Rio de Janeiro	3,300,000	22,000,000
British Empire	London	13,123,712	442,000,000
Bulgaria	Sofia	42,000	4,500,000
Canada	Ottawa	3,730,000	8,370,000
Chile	Santiago	295,000	4,000,000
China	Peking	4,300,000	400,000,000
Colombia	Bogota	462,000	5,475,000
Costa Rica	San Jose	23,000	441,000
Cuba	Havana	44,178	3,000,000
Czecho-Slovakia	Prague	56,300	14,000,000
Denmark	Copenhagen	15,500	3,000,000

Ecuador	Quito	116,530	1,300,000
Egypt	Cairo	363,181	12,800,000
England and Wales	London	50,874	46,000,000
Finland	Helsingfors	125,689	3,330,000
France	Paris	212,659	41,500,000
Germany	Berlin	172,000	55,000,000
Greece	Athens	41,933	5,000,000
Guatemala	New Guatemala	47,500	2,000,000
Haiti	Port au Prince	10,204	2,000,000
Holland	The Hague	12,761	6,600,000
Honduras	Teguciagalpa	44,275	553,446
Hungary	Budapest	62,000	10,000,000
India	Delhi	1,802,629	315,156,000
Ireland	Dublin	32,586	4,390,219
Italy	Rome	120,000	40,000,000
Japanese Empire	Tokyo	260,738	78,263,000
Jugo-Slavia	Belgrade	101,000	14,500,000
Lithuania	Vilna	23,500	2,000,000
Mexico	Mexico	769,000	16,000,000
Morocco	Fez	193,000	4,500,000
Nicaragua	Managua	51,700	600,000
Norway	Christiania	124,400	2,700,000
Panama	Panama	31,890	401,428
Paraguay	Asuncion	97,700	1,000,000
Persia	Teheran	630,000	10,000,000
Peru	Lima	680,026	3,530,000
Poland	Warsaw	142,000	30,000,000
Portugal	Lisbon	35,500	6,000,000
Roumania	Bucharest	122,000	15,000,000
Russia	Petrograd	8,300,000	167,000,000
Salvador	San Salvador	7,225	1,300,000
Santo Domingo	Santo Domingo	18,750	700,000
Scotland	Edinburgh	30,405	4,760,904
Siam	Bangkok	220,000	8,150,000
Spain	Madrid	196,700	20,500,000
Sweden	Stockholm	172,900	5,814,000
Switzerland	Berne	15,976	4,000,000
Turkey	Constantinople	174,900	8,000,000
Union of South Africa	Cape Town	467,701	6,000,000
United States	Washington	2,973,774	105,710,620
Uruguay	Montevideo	72,200	1,400,000
Venezuela	Caracas	393,976	2,848,000

Printing Presses.—There are three distinct classes of printing presses: (1) The ordinary job press which is used for the printing of cards, letter-heads, billheads, and other small matter. It is run by power or by a foot treadle. Each card or piece of paper is fed into the press by hand and removed by hand. The average speed is from 1,000 to 1,200 an hour, but the most expert feeders can handle about 1,500 cards an hour, and the record is not far from 2,000. (2) The cylinder press. This press is used for the printing of weekly newspapers, books, catalogues, and other large work. The type is placed upon a flat bed having a lateral movement, and the paper is fed by hand onto a cylinder which revolves over the moving bed. These presses have a speed of from 1,000 to 2,000 an hour, but comparatively few hand-feeders can handle more than 1,500, or 1,600 sheets in an hour. (3) The perfecting press. This press is used exclusively for the printing of large city newspapers, and some books, and catalogues are printed upon it. The type matter is cast into to a cylinder. The paper to be printed upon stereotypes of circular form which are attached is in a continuous roll and passes between the stereotype cylinder and another roller. The paper is fed into the press automatically, and is automatically folded and counted. The largest perfecting press in the world will print, fold, and count both sides of an eight-page paper at the rate of 300,000 copies an hour, but the average perfecting press does not deliver more than 75,000 copies an hour. The perfecting presses used for books, magazines, and catalogues run at a much slower speed.

Production of Books.—In 1921 8,329 books were produced in or imported into America of which 972 were fiction, 269 philosophy, 595 religion, 622 sociology, 191 law, 216 education, 673 science, 562 technical books, 299 medicine and hygiene, 169 agriculture, 267 business, 195 fine arts, 409 general literature, 512 poetry and drama, 576 juveniles, 572 history, 328 geography and travel, and 362 biography.

Public Debt of the United States.—The interest-bearing debt of the United States on July 1, 1920 was $24,061,095,361; the annual interest charge was about one billion dollars. The debt per capita was over $228; this was far greater than any previous debt in the country's history. In 1840 it was only 21 cents per capita.

Public Schools.—The public school system originated in Massachusetts and Connecticut shortly after the settlement of those States.

Pure Food.—Pure food laws enacted by the United States Government, and by State and City Governments, are supposed to protect the consumer against adulterated foods. The United States law, however, has no jurisdiction over food manufactured or put out in any of the States, unless it is carried from one State to another. The local food laws have to do only with the communities covered. The present law does not appear to be sufficient to protect the public fully. The statement written on many food packages, reading "Guaranteed Under The Food and Drugs Act, June 30, 1906. No. ——," must not be considered as proof positive of purity. It simply means that the contents of the package or bottle is according to the prescription or formula registered with the Government, and does not stand for quality or purity. Benzoate of soda and other preservatives may be legally used, provided [a statement to that effect is made upon the package. Chemists differ as to the injurious effect of benzoate of soda, but it is not advocated by any eminent authority. Most of the pure food experts are opposed to its use, irrespective of any injurious effect it may have upon the consumer, because this preservative will effectively kill the odor of putrefaction and disguise the taste and smell of rotten or spoiled fruit and other products. The consumer will do well to refuse to purchase any article or food containing benzoate of soda or other preservative, for first-class and healthy meat, fruit, and vegetables do not require a chemical preservative. Artificial coloring may not be injurious, as so little of it is required, but food artificially preserved may be dangerous, and very likely is impure, and may not have been fresh when canned.

Pyramids.—The pyramids were supposed to have been constructed between the fifth and twelfth dynasties in Middle Egypt, and not to have been used for tombs. They are built upon a square base, with sides facing the points of the compass, and the earlier pyramids were constructed of horizontal layers of rough blocks fastened together with mortar. In the center of the pyramid, near the base, was built a chamber reached by a passage from the north side. It is said that some of them contain emblems or symbols, which are now used in masonry. Whether or not there were masons at the time they were built, has not yet been discovered. Many of the stones weigh as much as thirty tons each, and no one has yet been able to ascertain the power used for their transmission.

Railroads.—The railroads of the United States employ nearly 2,000,000 men, or about 790 per hundred miles of track. The railroads occupy over 253,520 miles of track. The most powerful locomotive in the world runs in Virginia, and weighs 540,000 pounds. The heaviest electric locomotive is maintained by the Boston & Maine Railroad and weighs about 192,000 pounds. The most expensive locomotives cost about $37,000, and an ordinary locomotive costs from $15,000 to $20,000. An ordinary box car weighs 36,000 pounds, and a day coach about 112,000 pounds. Sleeping cars weigh from 115,000 to 152,000 pounds. The fastest short-distance run on record was made by the Empire State Express, at the rate of 112½ miles per hour. A New York train ran a distance of 44 miles in 33 minutes, or at the rate of 80 miles an hour, and a New York Central train made the distance between New York and Chicago, 965 miles, in 15 hours and 43 minutes, or at the rate of 62½ miles per hour. A New York Central train ran a short distance at the rate of about 112½ miles an hour, and a Florida train ran 5 miles at the rate of 120 miles an hour. There are annually over 5,000 accidents by collision and over 8,000 by derailment; in 1919 there were 301 passengers killed and 8,147 injured; 2,271 employees were killed and 131,211 injured; 4,406 persons not connected with the railroads and not riding on trains were killed, and 9,695 injured. The railroads of the United States carry over a billion passengers annually. They were under Federal control from Jan. 1, 1918 to Mar. 1, 1920, and were operated by the government at a loss of $900,478,766.

Referendum.—A law by which all legislation may be referred to the people, either for its ratification or rejection. The Initiative is a process by which any law may be enacted, if requested by a specified number of citizens.

The Initiative and Referendum are becoming common, and their advocates believe that they are the solution to many of our political problems.

Religious Denominations.—In the United States there are 114,000 Adventists, over 7,-000,000 Baptists, about 790,000 Congregationalists, about 1,226,000 Disciples of Christ, about 426,000 Lutherans, over 7,000,000 Methodists, about 2,275,000 Presbyterians, about 1,092,000 Protestant Episcopalians, about 367,-000 United Brethren, about 82,000 Unitarians, about 58,000 Universalists, and about 17,700,-000 Roman Catholics.

Roads.—The mileage of all public roads in the United States in 1920 was approximately 2,777,000 miles, of which about 300,000 miles was surfaced roads. About $200,000,000 were spent in construction and maintenance of roads during the year, over $11,730,000 by the Federal Government, over $106,860,000 by the States, and over $81,700,000 by local governments.

Round Table.—Tradition says that it was modeled after a table made by Joseph of Arimathea, and was an imitation of the one used at the Last Supper. It is said to have had a seating capacity variously estimated at from thirteen to one hundred and fifty. According to the legend dealing with King Arthur and his knights, it was a round marble table made by the Enchanter Merlin for Uther Pendragon. Later it came into the possession of the King of Camelard, and was given by him to Arthur on his marriage to the king's daughter Guinevere. The term Round Table is much used in the United States, and refers to a table, usually round, occupied habitually by the same diners.

Royal Academy.—Founded in London in 1768. It is an association of artists, and maintains a free school of art. It holds an annual exhibition of paintings and sculptures.

Royal Society.—One of the most celebrated associations in the world. Organized in London in 1660 for the promotion of scientific investigation.

School Statistics.—There are, in the United States, 30,000 men and 7,000 women acting as professors and instructors in universities, colleges, and technical schools. The common schools contain over 20,853,000 enrolled pupils, with an average daily attendance of over 15,-548,000. These schools employ over 105,000 men and 545,000 women as teachers. The estimated value of public school property is considerably more than $1,000,000,000, and the annual cost of maintaining these schools exceeds $763,000,000.

Seasickness.—Although there are several advertised remedies which claim to prevent or to cure seasickness, it is probable that none of them are efficacious for all persons. Seasickness is not perfectly understood. Some people suffer from it and some do not. Of course, the condition of the stomach and liver has much to do with it. If one is bilious he is pretty sure to become seasick. Before taking a voyage, it is well to diet or to live on plain food for a while. Do not remain in your stateroom or in the cabin. Get all of the fresh air you can. Lie down and don't refuse to eat sparingly. Many persons ward off seasickness by retiring before the vessel leaves the port. Some people, even sailors, suffer from seasickness with every voyage. A good remedy is an emetic, either warm salt water, or warm mustard water.

Seven Chief Virtues.—These, as defined by the Roman Cathoic Church, are as follows: (1) Faith, (2) Hope, (3) Charity, (4) Prudence, (5) Temperance, (6) Justice, (7) Fortitude.

Seven Corporal Works of Mercy.—According to the Roman Catholic Church, these are as follows: (1) To bury the dead, (2) to clothe the naked, (3) to feed the hungry, (4) to give drink to the thirsty, (5) to shelter the homeless, (6) to visit those in prison, (7) to administer unto the sick.

Seven Deadly Sins.—According to the teaching of the Roman Catholic Church, these are as follows: (1) Pride, (2) Anger, (3) Envy, (4) Sloth, (5) Lust, (6) Covetousness, (7) Gluttony.

Seven Liberal Arts.—A term applied during the Middle Ages to the following branches of learning: (1) Arithmetic, (2) Geometry, (3) Astronomy, (4) Music, (5) Logic, (6) Rhetoric, (7) Grammar.

Seven Spiritual Works of Mercy.—According to the teaching of the Roman Catholic Church, these are as follows: (1) To admonish the sinful, (2) to bear wrongs patiently, (3) to comfort the afflicted, (4) to counsel the doubting, (5) to forgive offenses, (6) to instruct the ignorant, (7) to pray for the living and the dead.

Seven Wise Men of Greece.—Applied to seven Greek sages, whose wisdom was embodied in the following maxims: (1) Solon of Athens, "Know thyself"; (2) Chilo of Sparta, "Consider the end"; (3) Thales of Miletus, "Suretyship brings ruin"; (4) Bias of Priene, "Most men are bad"; (5) Cleobulus of Lindus, "Avoid extremes"; (6) Pittacus of Mitylene, "Know thine opportunity"; (7) Periander of Corinth, "Nothing is impossible to industry."

Seven Wonders of the Middle Ages.—(1) The Coliseum at Rome, (2) the Catacombs of Alexandria, (3) the Great Wall of China, (4) the Leaning Tower of Pisa, (5) the Porcelain Tower of Nanking, (6) the Mosque of St.

Sophia at Constantinople, (7) the Ruins of Stonehenge.

Seven Wonders of the New World.—(1) Niagara Falls, (2) Yellowstone Park, (3) Garden of the Gods, (4) Mammoth Cave, (5) Yosemite Valley, (6) Giant Trees, (7) Natural Bridge.

Seven Wonders of the World.—In ancient times generally regarded as follows: (1) The Pyramids of Egypt, (2) the Hanging Gardens of Babylon, (3) the Mausoleum at Halicarnassus, (4) the Temple of Diana at Ephesus, (5) the Colossus of Rhodes, (6) the Pharos at Alexandria, (7) the Statue of the Olympian Jove in Elis.

Shaving Lotions.—Hot water applied to the face after shaving removes much of the sting or soreness, and the use of bay rum, hamamelis or witch hazel, or almond cream, is to be recommended. A very good shaving preparation is made of equal parts of bay rum and hamamelis.

Ship Bells

Time, A. M.		Time, A. M.		Time, A. M.	
1 Bell	12.30	1 Bell	4.30	1 Bell	8.30
2 Bells	1.00	2 Bells	5.00	2 Bells	9.00
3 "	1.30	3 "	5.30	3 "	9.30
4 "	2.00	4 "	6.00	4 "	10.00
5 "	2.30	5 "	6.30	5 "	10.30
6 "	3.00	6 "	7.00	6 "	11.00
7 "	3.30	7 "	7.30	7 "	11.30
8 "	4.00	8 "	8.00	8 "	Noon

Time, P. M.		Time, P. M.		Time, P. M.	
1 Bell......12.30		1 Bell....... 4.30		1 Bell....... 8.30	
2 Bells..... 1.00		2 Bells...... 5.00		2 Bells...... 9.00	
3 " 1.30		3 " 5.30		3 " 9.30	
4 " 2.00		4 " 6.00		4 " 10.00	
5 " 2.30		1 Bell....... 6.30		5 " 10.30	
6 " 3.00		2 Bells...... 7.00		6 " 11.00	
7 " 3.30		3 " 7.30		7 " 11.30	
8 " 4.00		4 " 8.00		8 " ....Midn't	

The work on shipboard is done by watches, the crew being mustered into two divisions, known as the Starboard Watch and Port Watch. The day begins at noon, and is divided into: Afternoon Watch, noon to 4 P. M.; First Dog Watch, 4 P. M. to 6 P. M.; Second Dog Watch, 6 P. M. to 8 P. M.; First Watch, 8 P. M. to Midnight; Middle Watch, 12 A. M. to 4 A. M.; Morning Watch, 4 A. M. to 8 A. M.; Forenoon Watch, 8 A. M. to noon.

Slavery.—Slavery is of a prehistoric origin, but was commercialized by the Romans, some of whom had as many as 10,000 slaves. In 1834, the British Colonies emancipated nearly 800,000 slaves, and the Civil War wiped slavery out of the United States. It does not now exist in any civilized nation.

Soap.—Many of the soaps upon the market are impure and even dangerous, and never should be used. Most of the standard white soaps, however, are pure and may be used freely. Cheap laundry soaps are not only impure, but injure the hands; and many of the highly perfumed soaps are hardly better than laundry soaps. Thoroughly good soap can be purchased at retail for not exceeding ten cents a cake, and for this price one can obtain really all there is in soap. Medicated soaps, except the antiseptic soaps recomended by physicians, have little or no value. The reader should purchase only the standard grade of soaps, and should never pay more than 25 cents a cake for any soap, because any price in excess of 25 cents is for perfume or represents exorbitant profit. Every physician is familiar with soap quality, and will gladly give you a list of reliable soaps without charge. There is no such thing as a complexion soap, except that all good soaps aid the complexion. There is no soap safe to use that removes pimples, or keeps pimples or other skin troubles from coming. Soap has only one value, and that is, its ability to assist water in cleansing the skin, except the antiseptic soaps, which may prevent contagion and which should be used by all who enter the sick-room. Ninety-nine per cent. of the expensive soaps are no better, save for their perfume, than soap sold at five or ten cents a cake.

Solar System

The Solar System, of which the earth is a part, consists of eight planets and the sun, so far as has been discovered. Astronomers have located 465 asteroids, which are small bodies floating in space and with apparently established orbits. From time to time, astronomers claim to have discovered a new planet, but its existence is not as yet accepted. The following table gives interesting information:

	Mean Distance of Earth from Sun, Millions of Miles	Sidereal Period, Days	Orbit, Velocity, Miles per Second	Mean Diameter, Miles
Sun	...	....	.....	866,400
Mercury	36.0	87.969	23 to 35	3,030
Venus	67.2	224.701	21.9	7,700
Earth	92.8	365.256	18.5	7,918
Mars	141.5	686.95	15.0	4,230
Jupiter	483.3	4332.58	8.1	86,500
Saturn	886.0	10759.22	6.0	71,000
Uranus	1781.9	30686.82	4.2	31,900
Neptune	2791.6	60181.11	3.4	34,800

Some Things Worth Knowing

The people of the earth speak 3,424 languages or dialects.

There are 640 acres in a square mile.

The ordinary flour barrel contains 196 pounds of flour.

What is known as a hand measure is 4 inches.

The sun is over 92,500,000 miles from the earth, and the nearest fixed star is 16,000,000,-000 miles from the earth.

The stock yards in Chicago, which are the largest in the world, have 20 miles of streets, and the same number of miles of water troughs, with 50 miles of feeding troughs, and 75 miles of drainage. The yards will accommodate over 20,000 cattle, 20,000 sheep, and 120,000 hogs at one time. They cost over $10,000,000.

The average person inhales 2,600 gallons of air per day.

Songs of the Civil War

(1) Battle Cry of Freedom.—George F. Root. "Yes, we'll rally round the flag, boys."

(2) Battle Flag of the Republic.—O. W. Holmes. "Flag of the heroes who left us their glory."

(3) Battle Hymn of the Republic.—Julia Ward Howe. "Mine eyes have seen the glory of the coming of the Lord."

(4) The Blue and the Gray.—Francis M. Finch. "By the flow of the inland river."

(5) Brave Boys Are They.—Henry C. Work. "Brave boys are they, gone at their country's call."

(6) Dixie (Southern). — Albert Pike. "Southrons, hear your country call you."

(7) Dixie (Northern).—T. M. Cooley. "Away down South where grows the cotton."

(8) John Brown's Body. "John Brown's body lies a-mould'ring in the grave."

(9) Just Before the Battle, Mother.— George F. Root. "Just before the battle, mother, I am thinking most of you."

(10) Marching Through Georgia.—Henry C. Work. "Bring the good old bugle, boys; we'll sing another song."

(11) Maryland, My Maryland (Southern).
—Joseph R. Randall. "The despot's heel is
on thy shore, Maryland, my Maryland."

(12) Oh, Wrap the Flag Around Me, Boys.
—R. Stewart Taylor.

(13) Tramp, Tramp, Tramp.—George F.
Root. "In the prison cell I sit."

(14) When Johnny Comes Marching Home.
—Louis Lambert.

(15) When This Cruel War Is Over.—
Charles C. Sawyer. "Dearest love, do you
remember?"

—Harper's "Book of Facts."

Spectacles and Glasses.—If you find it difficult to read, or your eyes become weak and
tired, the chances are you need proper glasses.
Don't attempt to fit them to yourself. Employ
a first-class optician or oculist, the latter if
the trouble appears to be serious.

Sporting Information

Baseball: Baseball became the National
Game in 1885, although it was played to some
extent as early as 1840. The first baseball
club was known as the New York Knicker-
bockers, which was organized in 1845, and the
first match game was played at Hoboken, N.
J., in 1846. The first rules governing baseball
were made in New York City, in 1857, and the
National Baseball League was formed in New
York City during the same year. The first

champion team was that of New York, in 1858, but it was not until 1868 that a salaried team was in existence. The National League was formed in 1876, and the American League in 1881.

ATTENDANCE AND RECEIPTS OF WORLD CHAMPIONSHIP SERIES SINCE 1903.

Yr.	Clubs.	G.	Attendance.	Receipts.
1903	Boston, A. L.–Pittsburgh, N. L.........	8	100,429	$50,000
1905	N. Y., N. L.–Athletics, A. L............	5	91,723	68,436
1906	White Sox, A. L.–Cubs, N. L...........	6	99,845	106,550
1907	Chicago, N. L.–Detroit, A. L...........	5	78,068	101,728
1908	Chicago, N. L.–Detroit, A. L...........	5	62,223	94,975
1909	Pittsburgh, N. L.–Detroit, A. L.........	7	145,295	188,302
1910	Athletics, A. L.–Chicago, N. L.........	5	125,222	173,980
1911	Athletics, A. L.–Giants, N. L	6	179,851	342.364
1912	Red Sox, A. L.–Giants, N. L...........	8	252,037	490,833
1913	Athletics, A. L.–Giants, N. L...........	5	150,992	325,980
1914	Boston, N. L.–Philadelphia, A. L......	4	111,009	226,739
1915	Boston, A. L.–Philadelphia, N. L......	5	143,351	320,361
1916	Boston, A. L.–Brooklyn, N. L..........	5	162,859	385,590
1917	Chicago, A. L.–N. Y., N. L............	6	186,654	425,878
1918	Boston, A. L.–Chicago, N. L..........	6	128,483	179,619
1919	Cincinnati, N. L.–Chicago, A. L........	8	236,928	722,414
1920	Cleveland, A. L.–Brooklyn, N. L........	7	174,349	564,800
1921	N. Y., N. L.–N. Y., A. L..............	8	269,976	900,233

Pennant winners of the National League are: Chicago 1876, Boston 1877, 1878, Providence 1879, Chicago 1880, 1881, 1882, Boston 1883, Providence 1884, Chicago 1885, 1886, Detroit 1887, New York 1888, 1889, Brooklyn 1890, Boston 1891, 1892, 1893, Baltimore 1894, 1895, 1896, Boston 1897, 1898, Brooklyn 1899, 1900, Pittsburgh 1901, 1902, 1903, New York 1904, 1905, Chicago 1906,

WORLD CHAMPIONSHIP SERIES.

Year.	Winners.	Games Won.	Losers.	Games Won.
1885	Chicago (N. L.)	3	St. Louis (A. A.)	3 tie
1886	St. Louis (A. A.)	4	Chicago (N. L.)	2
1887	Detroit (N. L.)	10	St. Louis (A. A.)	4
1888	New York (N. L.)	10	St. Louis (A. A.)	4
1889	New York (N. L.)	6	Brooklyn (A. A.)	3
1890	Louisville (N. L.)	3	Brooklyn (A. A.)	3 tie
1892	Boston (N. L.)	5	Cleveland (N. L.)	0
1894	New York (N. L.)	4	Baltimore (N. L.)	0
1895	Cleveland (N. L.)	4	Baltimore (N. L.)	1
1896	Baltimore (N. L.)	4	Cleveland (N. L.)	0
1897	Baltimore (N. L.)	4	Boston (N. L.)	1
1903	Boston (A. L.)	5	Pittsburgh (N. L.)	3
1905	New York (N. L.)	4	Philadelphia (A. L.)	1
1906	Chicago (A. L.)	4	Chicago (N. L.)	2
1907	Chicago (N. L.)	4	Detroit (A. L.)	0
1908	Chicago (N. L.)	4	Detroit (A. L.)	1
1909	Pittsburgh (N. L.)	4	Detroit (A. L.)	3
1910	Philadelphia (A. L.)	4	Chicago (N. L.)	1
1911	Philadelphia (A. L.)	4	New York (N. L.)	2
1912	Boston (A. L.)	4	New York (N. L.)	3 tie
1913	Philadelphia (A. L.)	4	New York (N. L.)	1
1914	Boston (N. L.)	4	Philadelphia (A. L.)	0
1915	Boston (A. L.)	4	Philadelphia (N. L.)	1
1916	Boston (A. L.)	4	Brooklyn (N. L.)	1
1917	Chicago (A. L.)	4	New York (N. L.)	2
1918	Boston (A. L.)	4	Chicago (N. L.)	2
1919	Cincinnati (N. L.)	5	Chicago (A. L.)	3
1920	Cleveland (A. L.)	5	Brooklyn (N. L.)	2
1921	New York (N. L.)	5	New York (A. L.)	3

1907, 1908, Pittsburgh 1909, Chicago 1910, New York 1911, 1912, 1913, Boston 1914, Philadelphia 1915, Brooklyn 1916, New York 1917, Chicago 1918, Cincinnati, 1919, Brooklyn 1920, New York 1921.

Pennant winners of the American League are: Philadelphia 1902, Boston 1903, 1904, Philadelphia 1905, Chicago 1906, Detroit 1907, 1908, 1909, Philadelphia 1910, 1911, Boston 1912, Philadelphia 1913, 1914, Boston 1915, 1916, Chicago 1917, Boston 1918, Chicago 1919, Cleveland 1920, New York 1921.

Endurance Records: 1,000 miles in 1,000 consecutive hours, walking 1 mile each hour, by Charles F. Morse, at Jackson, Mich., starting at 1 P. M., Jan. 11, 1897, and ending at 4 A. M., Feb. 22, 1897, track 39 laps to mile.

Greatest distance walked without a rest, 121 miles, 385 yds., by C. A. Harriman, California.

Walk from Atlantic to Pacific Ocean: John Ennis started with a plunge in the surf at Coney Island, N. Y., Monday, May 23, 1910, and arrived at the Cliff Hotel, San Francisco, August 24, 1910, and took a plunge in the ocean before a crowd of admirers. He lowered Weston's time by 25 days. Ennis, like Weston, did not walk on Sunday.

Prize Fighter Champions.—Heavyweights (over 158 lbs.)—1890-1892, John L. Sullivan; 1892-1897, James J. Corbett; 1897-1899, Robert Fitzsimmons; 1899-1906, James J. Jeffries;

1906-1908, Tommy Burns; 1908-1915, Jack Johnson; 1915-1918, Jess Willard; 1919-1921, Jack Dempsey.

Middleweights (158 lbs.)—1890-1897, Robert Fitzsimmons; 1897-1907, Tommy Ryan; 1907-1908, Stanley Ketchel; 1908, Bill Papke and Stanley Ketchel; 1908-1910, Stanley Ketchel; 1911-1913, claimed by Frank Klaus, Mike Gibbons, Ed McGoorty and Geo. Chip; 1914-1917, Al McCoy; 1917-1920, Mike O'Dowd; 1921, Johnny Wilson.

Welterweights (145 lbs.)—1890-1893, no recognized champion; 1894-1896, Tommy Ryan; 1896-1897, Kid McCoy; 1898-1900, Billy Smith; 1900, Rube Ferns; 1901, Matty Matthews and Rube Ferns; 1901-1904, Joe Walcott; 1904-1908, Dixie Kid; 1914-1916, Kid Graves; 1916, Jack Britton; 1917-1918, Ted (Kid) Lewis; 1919-1921, Jack Britton.

Lightweights (133 lbs.)—1890-1893, Jack McAuliffe; 1893-1899, Kid Lavigne; 1899-1902, Frank Erne; 1902-1908, Joe Gans; 1908-1910, Battling Nelson; 1910-1912, Ad Wolgast; 1912-1914, Willie Ritchie; 1914-1917, Freddie Welsh; 1917-1921, Benny Leonard.

Featherweights (122 lbs.)—1890-1892, no recognized champion; 1892-1897, George Dixon; 1897, Solly Smith; 1898, Solly Smith and Dave Sullivan; 1898-1900, George Dixon; 1900-1901, Terry McGovern; 1901-1904, Young Corbett; 1904-1908, Tommy Sullivan; 1908-1911, Abe Attell; 1911-1921, Johnny Kilbane.

Bantamweights (116 lbs.) — 1890-1892, George Dixon; 1892-1894, no recognized champion; 1894-1898, Jimmy Barry; 1898-1901, no recognized champion; 1901-1903, Harry Forbes; 1903-1905, Frankie Neil; 1905-1907, no recognized champion; 1907-1913, Johnny Coulon; 1914-1915, Kid Williams; 1916-1920, Pete Herman; 1920-1921, Joe Lynch; 1921, Pete Herman, Johnny Buff.

Golf Champions

AMERICAN GOLF CHAMPIONS

Year.	National Open.	National Amateur.	Nat'l Women's Amateur.
1894	W. Dunn..........	W. G. Lawrence....	....
1895	H. Rawlins........	C. B. M'donald.....	Mrs. C. S. Brown.
1896	Jos. Foulis........	H. J. Whigham.....	Beatrix Hoyt.
1897	Jos. Floyd.........	H. J. Whigham.....	Beatrix Hoyt.
1898	Fred. Herd........	F. S. Douglas......	Beatrix Hoyt.
1899	W. Smith..........	H. M. Harriman....	Ruth Underhill.
1900	H'y Vardon.......	W. J. Travis.......	F. C. Griscom.
1901	W. Anderson......	W. J. Travis.......	Genev. Hecker.
1902	L. Auchterlonie....	L. N. James........	Genev. Hecker.
1903	W. Anderson......	W. J. Travis.......	Bess. Anthony.
1904	W. Anderson......	H. C. Egan........	Georg. Bishop.
1905	W. Anderson......	H. C. Egan........	Paul. MacKay.
1906	Alex. Smith.......	E. M. Byers........	Har. S. Curtis.
1907	Alex. Ross........	J. D. Travers......	Marg. Curtis.
1908	Fred. McLeod.....	J. D. Travers......	Cath. C. Harley.
1909	Geo. Sargent......	R. A. Gardner......	Dor. Campbell.
1910	Alex. Smith.......	W. C. Fownes......	Dor. Campbell.
1911	J. J. McDermott....	H. H. Hilton.......	Marg. Curtis.
1912	J. J. McDermott....	J. D. Travers......	Marg. Curtis.
1913	Fr. Ouimet........	J. D. Travers......	Glad. R'nscroft.
1914	W. C. Hagen......	Fr. Ouimet........	Mrs. H. Jackson.
1915	J. D. Travers......	R. A. Gardner.....	Mrs. C. V'rbeck.
1916	Ch. Evans, Jr.....	Ch. Evans, Jr.....	Alexa Stirling.
1917	J. Hutchison......	No match..........	No match.
1918	No match..........	No match..........	No match.
1919	W. C. Hagen......	S. D. Herron......	Alexa Stirling.
1920	Edw. Ray.........	C. Evans, Jr......	Alexa Stirling.
1921	Jas. Barnes........	T. Guilford........	M. Hollins.

BRITISH OPEN

Yr.	Winner.	Yr.	Winner.	Yr.	Winner.
1860	W. Parke, Sr.	1880	R. Ferguson.	1900	J. H. Taylor.
1861	T. Morris, Sr.	1881	R. Ferguson.	1901	J. Braid.
1862	T. Morris, Sr.	1882	R. Ferguson.	1902	A. Herd.
1863	W. Parke, Sr.	1883	W. Fernie.	1903	Hy. Vardon.
1864	T. Morris, Sr.	1884	J. Simpson.	1904	J. White.
1865	A. Strath.	1885	R. Martin.	1905	J. Braid.
1866	W. Parke, Sr.	1886	D. Brown.	1906	J. Braid.
1867	T. Morris, Sr.	1887	W. Parke, Jr.	1907	A. Massy.
1868	T. Morris, Jr.	1888	J. Burns.	1908	J. Braid.
1869	T. Morris, Jr.	1889	W. Parke, Jr.	1909	J. H. Taylor.
1870	T. Morris, Jr.	1890	J. Ball.	1910	J. Braid.
1871	No match.	1891	H. Kirkaldy.	1911	Hy. Vardon.
1872	T. Morris, Jr.	1892	H. H. Hilton.	1912	E. Ray.
1873	T. Kidd.	1893	W. Auchterlonie.	1913	J. H. Taylor.
1874	Mungo Park.	1894	J. H. Taylor.	1914	Hy. Vardon.
1875	W. Parke, Sr.	1895	J. W. Taylor.	1919	....
1876	R. Martin.	1896	Hy. Vardon.	1920	Geo. Duncan.
1877	J. Anderson.	1897	H. H. Hilton.	1921	J. Hutchison.
1878	J. Anderson.	1898	Hy. Vardon.		
1879	J. Anderson.	1899	Hy. Vardon.		

BRITISH AMATEURS

Yr.	Winner.	Yr.	Winner.	Yr.	Winner.
1886	H. Hutchison.	1897	A. J. T. Allan.	1908	E. A. Lassen.
1887	H. Hutchison.	1898	F. G. Tait.	1909	R. Maxwell.
1888	J. Ball, Jr.	1899	J. Ball, Jr.	1910	J. Ball.
1889	J. E. Laidlay.	1900	H. H. Hilton.	1911	H. H. Hilton.
1890	J. Ball, Jr.	1901	H. H. Hilton.	1912	J. Ball.
1891	J. E. Laidlay.	1902	C. Hutchings.	1913	H. H. Hilton.
1892	J. Ball, Jr.	1903	R. Maxwell.	1914	J. L. C. Jenkins.
1893	Peter Anderson.	1904	W. J. Travis.	1919	....
1894	J. Ball, Jr.	1905	A. G. Barry.	1920	C. Tolley.
1895	L. B. Melville.	1906	Jas. Robb.	1921	W. Hunter.
1896	F. G. Tait.	1907	J. Ball, Jr.		

BRITISH WOMEN'S

Yr.	Winner.	Yr.	Winner.	Yr.	Winner.
1893	Lady Marg. Scott	1902	May Hezlet.	1910	E. Grant-Suttle.
1894	Lady Marg. Scott.	1903	Rhona Adair.	1911	Dor. Campbell.
1895	Lady Marg. Scott.	1904	Lottie Dod.	1912	G. Ravencroft.
1896	Amy Pascoe.	1905	Ber. Thompson.	1913	Muriel Dodd.
1897	Edith Orr.	1906	Mrs. Kennion.	1914	Cecil Leitch.
1898	L. Thomson.	1907	May Hezlet.	1919	....
1899	May Hecht.	1908	Miss Titterton.	1920	Cecil Leitch.
1900	Rhona Adair.	1909	Dor. Campbell.	1921	Cecil Leitch.
1901	M. Graham.				

TENNIS CHAMPIONS OF U. S. IN SINGLES (OUTDOOR).
WOMEN CHAMPIONS.

Yr.	Champion.	Doubles Champions.
1900	Miss Murtle McAteer....	Misses E. Parker & H. Champlin.
1901	Miss Elizabeth H. Moore	Misses M. McAteer & J. P. Atkinson.
1902	Miss Marion Jones......	Misses M. Jones & J. P. Atkinson.
1903	Miss Elizabeth H. Moore	Misses E. H. Moore & C. B. Neely.
1904	Miss May Sutton........	Misses M. Sutton & M. Hall.
1905	Miss Elizabeth H. Moore	Misses H. H. Homans & C. B. Neely.
1906	Miss Helen H. Homans..	Mrs. L. F. Coe & Mrs. D. F. Platt.
1907	Miss Evelyn Sears......	Misses Neely & Weimer.
1908	Mrs. Barger Wallach....	Misses E. Sears & M. Curtis.
1909	Miss Hazel Hotchkiss....	Misses H. Hotchkiss & E. Rotch.
1910	Miss Hazel Hotchkiss....	Misses E. Rotch & H. Hotchkiss.
1911	Miss Hazel Hotchkiss....	Misses E. Sears and H. Hotchkiss.
1912	Miss Mary Browne......	Misses M. Browne & D. Green.
1913	Miss Mary Browne......	Miss M. Browne & Mrs. R. H. Williams.
1914	Miss Mary Browne......	Miss M. Browne & Mrs. R. H. Williams.
1915	Miss Molla Bjurstedt....	Mrs. G. W. Wightman & Miss El. Sears.
1916	Miss Molla Bjurstedt....	Misses M. Bjurstedt & E. Sears.
1917	Miss Molla Bjurstedt....	Misses M. Bjurstedt & E. Sears.
1918	Miss Molla Bjurstedt....	Misses E. Goss & M. Zinderstein.
1919	Mrs. Geo. W. Wightman.	Misses E. Goss & M. Zinderstein.
1920	Mrs. F. I. Mallory......	Misses E. Goss & M. Zinderstein.
1921	Mrs. F. I. Mallory......	Miss M. Browne & Mrs. L. R. Williams.

TENNIS CHAMPIONS OF U. S. IN SINGLES (OUTDOOR)

Yr.	Winner.	Yr.	Winner.	Yr.	Winner.
1881	R. D. Sears.	1895	F. H. Hovey.	1909	W. A. Larned.
1882	R. D. Sears.	1896	R. D. Wrenn.	1910	W. A. Larned.
1883	R. D. Sears.	1897	R. D. Wrenn.	1911	W. A. Larned.
1884	R. D. Sears.	1898	M. D. Whitman.	1912	M.E.McLoughlin
1885	R. D. Sears.	1899	M. D. Whitman.	1913	M.E.McLoughlin
1886	R. D. Sears.	1900	M. D. Whitman.	1914	R. N. Williams.
1887	H. W. Slocum.	1901	W. A. Larned.	1915	W. M. Johnston.
1888	H. W. Slocum.	1902	W. A. Larned.	1916	R. N. Williams.
1889	H. W. Slocum.	1903	H. L. Doherty.	1917	R. L. Murray.
1890	O. S. Campbell.	1904	H. Ward.	1918	R. L. Murray.
1891	O. S. Campbell.	1905	B. C. Wright.	1919	W. M. Johnston.
1892	O. S. Campbell.	1906	W. J. Clothier.	1920	W. T. Tilden, 2d.
1893	R. D.Wrenn.	1907	W. A. Larned.	1921	*W.T. Tilden, 2d.
1894	R. D. Wrenn.	1908	W. A. Larned.		

* Tilden defeated Wallace Johnson, 6—1, 6—3, 6—1, in final round.

Standard Time

Until 1883, each city or district maintained its own time, usually accepting what is known as True Time. This condition caused complications. For example: Many railroad-station clocks either gave two times, or else there were separate clocks for each time, some of the trains leaving the station on what was known as New York time, while others left on local time. Banks and business houses closed on either of the times. There was no standard and no agreement.

In 1883, Standard Time was established.

United States standard Eastern time is used from the Atlantic Ocean to a line through Sandusky and Mansfield, and between Columbus and Zanesville, Ohio; thence through Huntington, W. Va.; Norton, Va.; Johnson City, Tenn.; Asheville, N. C.; Atlanta and Macon, Ga., and Apalachicola, Fla. U. S. standard Central time is used from this first line to a line through Mandan, N. D.; Pierre, S. D.; McCook, Neb.; Dodge City, Kan., and along west line of Okla. and Tex.; standard Mountain time is used from the second line to a line that forms the western boundary of Montana, and thence passes through Pocatello, Idaho; Ogden and Salt Lake City, Utah; Parker and Yuma, Ariz. U. S. Standard

Pacific time is used from the third line to the Pacific Ocean.

There is a difference of just one hour between the sections. When it is 12 o'clock at Boston, Mass., or at New York City, it is 11 o'clock at Chicago, and at San Francisco 9 o'clock.

The changing from so-called Local or True Time to Standard Time required clocks at Boston to be set back 16 minutes; New York clocks to be set back 4 minutes; Detroit clocks to be set back 28 minutes; St. Louis clocks to be moved ahead one minute; and San Francisco clocks to be set ahead ten minutes.

Standard Time was made the legal time throughout the United States by an act of Congress, approved March 19, 1918. The Canadian Pacific Railroad, which has the longest mileage of any railroad in the world, is run on what is known as the 24-Hour Time; that is, the faces of its clocks, instead of bearing the figures 1 to 12, run from 1 to 24 inclusive. The time-tables are rather confusing, as trains are billed to arrive and depart at 13:10, 16:14, 23:30, etc. This system appears to have only one advantage,—that it eliminates the use of A. M. and P. M. It is possible that it will be accepted elsewhere, and even generally, but not for the present.

Star Chamber.—A tribunal, made up of a committee of the King's Privy Council, instituted or revived in 1486. It was supposed to have almost unlimited powers and to be exempt from any rules or law. It had the right to inflict any form of punishment except death. The term is now applied to assemblies or committees or others who conduct their investigations and decide upon questions in secret.

Stars, Their Number

The number of visible stars is as follows:

19	stars	of	the	first	magnitude
59	"	"	"	second	"
182	"	"	"	third	"
530	"	"	"	fourth	"
1,600	"	"	"	fifth	"
4,800	"	"	"	sixth	"
13,000	"	"	"	seventh	"
40,000	"	"	"	eighth	"
100,000	"	"	"	ninth	"
400,000	"	"	"	tenth	"
1,000,000	"	"	"	eleventh	"
3,000,000	"	"	"	twelfth	"
10,000,000	"	"	"	thirteenth	"
30,000,000	"	"	"	fourteenth	"
56,000,000	"	"	"	fifteenth	"

100,560,190

Star-Spangled Banner.—The national song

of the United States. Composed by Francis Scott Key on the night of September 13, 1814. " The cartel-ship *Minden* was anchored in sight of Fort McHenry, and from her deck Key saw, during the night of 13 Sept., 1814, the bombardment of that fortress. It was during the excitement of this attack, and while pacing the deck of the *Minden* with intense anxiety between midnight and dawn, that Key composed the song. It was first written on the back of a letter, and after his return to Baltimore copied out in full."—Harper's " Book of Facts."

Statistics of Population—United States, by States

POPULATION OF CONTINENTAL UNITED STATES, BY DIVISIONS AND STATES, 1910 AND 1920 AND RANK IN POPULATION

Geographic Division and State	Population 1920	Population 1910	Rank in Population 1920	Rank in Population 1910
Continental United States	105,710,620	91,972,266	....	....
GEOGRAPHIC DIVISIONS:				
New England	7,400,909	6,552,681	VII	VII
Middle Atlantic	22,261,144	19,315,892	I	I
East North Central	21,475,543	18,250,621	II	II
West North Central	12,544,249	11,637,921	IV	IV
South Atlantic	13,990,272	12,194,895	III	III
East South Central	8,893,307	8,409,901	VI	VI
West South Central	10,242,224	8,784,534	V	V
Mountain	3,336,101	2,633,517	IX	IX
Pacific	5,566,871	4,192,304	VIII	VIII
NEW ENGLAND:				
Maine	768,014	742,371	35	34
New Hampshire	443,083	430,572	41	39
Vermont	352,428	335,956	45	42
Massachusetts	3,852,356	3,366,416	6	6
Rhode Island	604,397	542,610	38	38
Connecticut	1,380,631	1,114,756	29	31
MIDDLE ATLANTIC:				
New York	10,385,227	9,113,614	1	1
New Jersey	3,155,900	2,537,167	10	11
Pennsylvania	8,720,017	7,665,111	2	2

EAST NORTH CENTRAL:

Ohio	5,759,394	4,157,545	4	4
Indiana	2,930,390	2,516,462	11	9
Illinois	6,485,280	4,821,550	3	3
Michigan	3,668,412	2,420,982	7	8
Wisconsin	2,632,067	2,069,042	13	13

WEST NORTH CENTRAL:

Minnesota	2,387,125	2,075,708	17	19
Iowa	2,404,021	2,224,771	16	15
Missouri	3,404,055	3,293,335	9	7
North Dakota	646,872	577,056	36	37
South Dakota	636,547	583,888	37	36
Nebraska	1,296,372	1,192,214	31	29
Kansas	1,769,257	1,690,949	24	22

SOUTH ATLANTIC:

Delaware	223,003	202,322	47	47
Maryland	1,449,661	1,295,346	28	27
District of Columbia	437,571	331,069	42	43
Virginia	2,309,187	2,061,612	20	20
West Virginia	1,463,701	1,221,119	27	28
North Carolina	2,559,123	2,206,287	14	16
South Carolina	1,683,724	1,515,400	26	26
Georgia	2,895,832	2,609,121	12	10
Florida	968,470	752,619	32	33

EAST SOUTH CENTRAL:

Kentucky	2,416,630	2,289,905	15	14
Tennessee	2,337,885	2,184,789	19	17
Alabama	2,348,174	2,138,093	18	18
Mississippi	1,790,618	1,797,114	23	21

WEST SOUTH CENTRAL:

Arkansas	1,752,204	1,574,449	25	25
Louisiana	1,798,509	1,656,388	22	24
Oklahoma	2,028,283	1,657,155	21	23
Texas	4,663,228	3,896,542	5	5

MOUNTAIN:

Montana	548,889	376,053	39	40
Idaho	431,866	325,594	43	45
Wyoming	194,402	145,965	48	48
Colorado	939,629	799,024	33	32
New Mexico	360,350	327,301	44	44
Arizona	334,162	204,354	46	46
Utah	449,396	373,351	40	41
Nevada	77,407	81,875	49	49

PACIFIC:

Washington	1,356,621	1,141,990	30	30
Oregon	783,389	672,765	34	35
California	3,426,861	2,377,549	8	12

Stature and Weights

There have appeared in public print, several tables, which, the compilers claim, are based upon Greek and other measurements. It is probable that few of these tables are authentic, and many of them are, undoubtedly, incorrect. The following table is compiled by Jay W. Seaver, M. D., for 20 years professor at Yale University, and is as nearly correct as possibility would admit. Dr. Seaver, however, does not claim absolute correctness. The second and third tables given are used quite generally in civil service examinations by local, state, and national governments, and apply largely to those seeking positions on the police force or the fire department.

Height, Feet	Males—Weight.		Females—Weight.	
	Fat	Normal	Fat	Normal
5	136	112	122	102
5.1	141	116	128	106
5.2	146	120	134	109
5.3	152	125	140	113
5.4	160	130	145	117
5.5	167	135	151	121
5.6	175	138	154	125
5.7	182	140	157	130
5.8	189	143	160	135
5.9	196	150	169	140
5.10	203	155	173	145
5.11	210	160	179	150
6	216	165	185	155
6.1	221	170	187	160
6.2	226	175	196	166
6.3	231	180	205	171

Minimum circumference of the Chest tolerable in applicants.

Height		Circumference of Chest	Height		Circumference of Chest
Feet	Inches	Inches	Feet	Inches	Inches
5	6	32½	5	11	35½
5	7	33	6	..	36
5	7½	33½	6	1	36½
5	8	34	6	2	37
5	9	34½	6	3	37¼
5	10	35	6	4	38

The stature shall not be below 5 ft. 6 in., nor the weight below that marked as its minimum accompaniment in the subjoined table.

Height		Min.	Average	Max. Weight
Feet	Inches	Pounds	Pounds	Pounds
5	6	136	143	180
5	7	138	146	187
5	8	140	148	195
5	9	145	155	202
5	10	150	160	210
5	11	155	165	217
6	..	160	170	225
6	1	165	175	233
6	2	170	180	240
6	3	175	185	248

Steam Engine.—The principle of the steam engine is very simple. Stripped of all technicality, it may be described as follows: Take a can with a height somewhat longer than its width, and close up both ends. Make a hole in the center of one of the ends large enough for the insertion of a rod about the diameter of a small poker. Fasten one end of this rod to the center of a disc which will fit closely into the can. Insert this disc in the can with the poker passing through the hole. The whole apparatus will be similar to that of a churn. Bore two holes in the sides of the can, at top and bottom. Allow steam to pass into the can through the first hole, which will force the disc to the other end of the can, and draw the poker with it. Then, introduce steam through the other hole. This will drive the disc to the other end of the can, and at the same time the steam entering the first hole will pass out. This gives a motion to the poker rod, which continues so long as steam is forced in and out. The rod, is, of course, connected with a crank which works on a shaft, and from this shaft power is transmitted. The steam is let into the cylinder automatically. A fly wheel is maintained where there is not more than one cylinder, and even where there is more than one, so as to create momentum, which carries the crank beyond its dead center. The modern steam engine makes from 100 to even 1,000 revolutions a minute. Its power is measured by its capacity to equal that of one or several horses, and is known as horse-power. Steam engines are made with a capacity of only a small fraction of horse-power, and up to several thousand. But usually, where great power is required, more than one cylinder is used, all of them working upon the same shaft. The so-called turbine steam engine is similar to the ordinary turbine water wheel, except that steam, instead of water, is forced against it. See " Turbines."

Strikes.—The strike is an agreement upon the part of workmen to refuse to work until their demands are accepted. The first strike in the United States took place in New York City, in 1803, and was confined to sailors. In 1888, there were 697 strikes, involving over 210,000 employees. In 1886, the number of strikes increased 52 per cent., and in 1888 the increase was 22 per cent. There were 3,681 strikes in 1916; 4,324 in 1917; 3,248 in 1918; 3,444 in 919; and 3,109 in 1920. Each year the largest number of strikes occurs in the State of New York.

Sub Rosa.—The term "under the rose" implies secrecy. It had its origin B. C. 477, when Pausanias, commander of the fleet of Spartans and Athenians, was intriguing with Xerxes for the subjugation of Greece to Persia and for the hand of the king's daughter in marriage. The business was transacted in the "Brazen House," the roof of , which was a garden making a bower of roses. Hence the term Sub Rosa.

Sugar Industry.—The United States consumes each year nearly 3,500,000 tons of sugar, or about 80 pounds per capita.

Sunday Schools.—The Sunday Schools of the United States have about 19,935,000 scholars and 1,952,000 officers and teachers. The Sunday School membership of England and Wales is over 7,000,000. Connected with the Sunday Schools of the world are about 2,650,000 teachers and 26,500,000 scholars.

Talking Machines.—The talking machine, known by several names, including the phonograph, was originally invented by Edison. Unscientifically speaking, it consists of a disc similar to that used in the telephone, with a needle or point attached to the center of the underside of it. This needle or point fits into circular or cylindrical grooves, which are covered with tin foil or other malleable substance.

The vibrations of the voice or of music, which reach the disc, cause this needle or point to rise or fall, producing impressions upon the tin foil or other substance. After the record has been made, duplicates are produced in a substance largely made of rubber, which is placed on a rotary disc or cylinder that is turned automatically, the needle or point attached to the disc working into the grooves and rising with or following the impressions, which cause the plate or disc to vibrate. The process is wholly mechanical, and electricity is not used.

Tariff.—This word, meaning a schedule of duties on merchandise, imported or exported, is said to come from Tarifa, a town in Southern Spain, on the Mediterranean Sea, where duties were once levied by the Moors on all ships passing in or out of the Straits of Gibraltar.

Telegraph.—The conception of the telegraph came to Professor Morse, in 1832, while he was making a voyage from Europe to America, and he at once began his experiments, which resulted in what may be considered one of the two greatest inventions or discoveries. After waiting about eight years, Congress reluctantly appropriated a sum sufficient to build a telegraph line between Washington and Baltimore. The original conception of telegraphy belongs wholly to Professor Morse, but since its invention other scientists have invented improvements, including an apparatus which allows the sending of two messages each way, or four messages in all, over the same wire at the same time. The telegraphic code or alphabet, originally invented by Morse, remains practically intact. It consists of dots and dashes, and may be learned in a few hours, although expertness requires a year or more of practice. Unscientifically speaking, the telegraphic apparatus is extremely simple: it consists primarily of a piece of soft iron around which is wound several strands of insulated wire. During the time that electricity is passing through this wire. the soft iron becomes a magnet, but returns to its nonmagnetic character when electricity is not passing around it. A battery is used for the generating of electricity. The operator turns electricity into the wire by pressing a key. When the key is down, the electricity passes around the piece of soft iron and makes of it a magnet, which will draw iron or steel to it, the same as does any ordinary permanent magnet. Just above the end of the soft iron is placed a piece of metal, and as the key is pressed letting in the electricity, the iron (then a magnet) draws this metal to it, producing a slight sound or click. This piece of iron is held by a spring, and springs back into place when electricity is let out of the insulated wire surrounding the soft iron. If a message is to be sent a long distance, a relay is used so as to turn into the wire additional currents of electricity, because electricity loses some of its strength if carried over a very long wire, and a relay adds new or fresh currents from separate batteries. In this way, a message can be sent continuously for several thousand miles, which would be impossible without the use of relays. The process of sending several messages at the same time over the same wire is somewhat complicated. The result is obtained by using currents of electricity of different intensity, the currents not interfering with each other. The ocean cables are described under another heading.

Telephone.—The telephone is supposed to have been invented by Professor A. G. Bell, in 1875, but scientists recognize the probable invention of it, largely in theory, by the eminent scientists Dolbear, Gray, Edison, and possibly others. It is exceedingly difficult to describe, other than scientifically, the working of the telephone; and it cannot be done perfectly until electricity is fully understood. We know the result, but are not able to locate all of the causes. The original telephone consisted of a bar of magnetized steel of about the circumference of an ordinary poker, a few inches in length, around which was wound insulated wire. At one end of the magnet, and close to it, was placed a metallic disc about twice the circumference of a silver dollar and of the thickness of thin tin. Originally the same instrument was used both for sending and for receiving. Any sound, including the human voice, brought in direct contact with the disc, caused it to vibrate, and for some unknown reason these vibrations were transmitted through the magnet, and by the wires carried to another similar instrument. The sounds and voice were carried a short distance without the use of a battery, and the early telephones had ground circuits; that is, there was only one wire between the stations, the other wire being grounded by being attached to gas or other pipes, the electricity making half the circuit through the earth. Later on a battery was used, which increased the sending distances, but the ground wire remained for some time. The present telephone consists of the original telephone as a receiver, but with a transmitter into which the sender speaks his words. The mechanism of the transmitter is complicated and cannot be described except scientifically. Conversations now extend from coast to coast and farther with perfect distinctness. Non-technically speaking, then, the telephone consists of a magnet, insulated wire, and a disc, the vibration upon the disc being transmitted over the wire from the sending to the receiving station, electricity being used for conveying the vibrations or sound.

Over twelve billion conversations were held in this country in 1921 over the wires of the American Telephone and Telegraph Co., according to its annual report. The daily average was 33,162,000. There were over 8,333,-000 telephones operated by this company and over 4,267,000 connected telephones owned by other companies, making a total of over 12,-600,000 telephones in use in 1921.

Ten Great Religions.—James Freeman Clarke, in his book "Ten Great Religions," gives the following as the ten most important faiths of ancient and modern times:

(1) Confucianism.
(2) Brahmanism.
(3) Buddhism.
(4) Zoroastrianism.
(5) Religion of Egypt.
(6) Religion of Greece and Rome.
(7) Teutonic and Scandinavian Religion.
(8) Judaism.
(9) Christianity.
(10) Islâm.

Théâtre Français.—The most famous theatre in Paris, and, perhaps, in the world. It is situated in the Place du Palais Royal, and is the home of the Comédie Française. In 1900 it was destroyed by fire, but immediately rebuilt. The original building was erected in 1782, but was later much altered.

Thunder.—The sound of thunder is produced by the sudden rush of the air into the vacuum caused by the rapid passage of lightning through the air.

Ticket-of-Leave.—The English Government in 1854 issued a permit which allowed a convict his liberty before the expiration of his term. It was necessary for him to report to the police at stated times, and, if he committed any crime, his ticket-of-leave was recalled. The ticket-of-leave is similar to probation granted in the United States.

Time Difference.—When it is 12 o'clock

noon in New York City, it is 5:13 in Antwerp; about 5:49 in Berlin; about 5:13 in Brussels; about 1:02 in Buenos Ayres; about 10:49 in Calcutta; about 6:53 in Constantinople; about 4:30 in Dublin; about 4:34 in Liverpool; about 4:56 in London; about 5:05 in Paris; about 5:46 in Rome; about 6:57 in St. Petersburg. When it is 12 o'clock noon in New York City, it is 33½ minutes earlier in Havana; about 11 hours and 28 minutes earlier in Hong Kong; about 9 hours and 24 minutes earlier in Melbourne; about 9 hours and 45½ minutes earlier in Yokohama.

Tobacco Industry.—The United States grows about 1,508,000,000 pounds of tobacco a year, and over a million acres are used for growing tobacco. The value of the tobacco grown each year is about $318,200,000.

To Estimate the Weight of Hay.—Find the length, breadth, and depth of the hay, in feet, and multiply these three dimensions together; if the hay is on the wagon or newly stored, divide the product by 540; but if it is well settled in the mow or stack, divide by 512. If the hay is baled, 270 cubic feet will weigh a ton. The number of cubic feet in a circular stack is found by multiplying the average circumference in yards by itself and this product by four times the height of the stack in yards; then point off the two right-hand figures and multiply the result by 27.

To Find Length of Day or Night.—At any

time of the year add 12 hours to the time of
the sun's setting, and from the sum subtract
the time of rising for the length of the day.
Subtract the time of setting from 12 hours,
and to the remainder add the time of rising
next morning for the length of the night.
These rules are equally true for apparent
time.

To Measure Corn in the Crib.—Find the
length, breadth, and depth of the corn, in feet,
and multiply these three dimensions together;
this product multiplied by .63 will give the
number of heaped bushels in the ear. Sometimes one and one-half bushels of ears make
a bushel of shelled corn, and sometimes it requires two bushels, the amount required de-
pending upon the size of the cob, shape of
the ear, etc.

Tom Thumb.—Tom Thumb was probably
the most famous dwarf in the world, not because of the absence of others of the same
height, or less, but because he was exploited
by the late P. T. Barnum. Tom Thumb,
whose real name was Charles S. Stratton, was
born in 1838, and died in 1883. In 1842 he was
two feet in height and weighed sixteen pounds.
In 1863 his height increased to thirty-one
inches, and later to forty inches.

To Produce Different Colors.—The color
printed in *italics* may be made by mixing the
other two colors. *Purple,* red with light blue.

Brown, red with black. *Rose,* lake with white. *Drab,* umber with white. *Chestnut,* white with brown. *Chocolate,* yellow with brown. *Flesh Color,* carmine with straw. *Pearl,* blue with lead color. *Pink,* carmine with white. *Silver Gray,* lamp black with indigo. *Lead Color,* lamp black with white. *Bright Green,* Paris green with white. *Buff,* yellow ochre with white. *French White,* white tinted with purple. *Dark Green,* black with chrome green. *Brilliant Green,* emerald green with white. *Pea Green,* chrome green with white. *Orange,* vermillion with chrome yellow. *Straw Color,* chrome yellow with white lead. *Cream Color,* white tinted with red and yellow. *Ashes of Roses,* white with tints of black and purple. *French Gray,* white tinted with black and purple. *Olive,* chrome yellow, blue, and black with red.

Trade Unions.—The trade union, although supposed to be of modern origin, was established as early as 1548. Mythical history which, of course, cannot be authenticated, indicates the possibility of an organization of working men at the time of the building of Solomon's temple. During the last several years, trade unionism has grown to enormous proportions, and practically every vocation has its union or organization. The right to organize is self-evident, so long as it does not restrain trade or interfere with personal rights. The employee and employer certainly have legal and moral rights to do as they please, provided they do not interfere with

legal or moral law, and do not use coercion.
Moral influence, however, cannot be criticised.
The maintenance of a well-organized labor
union is to the advantage of both capital and
labor, and should be encouraged. Naturally,
the binding together of laborers or workmen,
and that of capital, causes some abuses, for
humanity, as it runs, is not always fair; but
one should not criticise either side without
criticising the other. Both have their advantages and disadvantages, both are fair and unfair. As civilization progresses, the mistakes
and abuses will be corrected, and organized
labor and capital will work in harmony.

Trusts.—A trust is an association of capi-
talists, organized for the purpose of control-
ing any one trade or trades. It is illegal and
may be punished by imprisonment or fine.
It is exceedingly difficult, however, to discover
whether or not an organization is in actual
restraint of trade, and to prosecute a combination. Undoubtedly trusts exist in America,
and all over the world for that matter, and are
illegal. Great effort is being made to dis-
band them, but so far has very little real effect, for most of the trusts which are dis-
organized by law continue in some other form.

Turbines.—The turbine has largely taken
the place of the water wheel, because it is
more compact, produces greater energy, and
is more powerful. It is, untechnically speak-

ing, a box containing a series of fanlike blades set at an angle, so that water or steam brought against them will make them turn.

Type.—Movable metallic type was invented by Gutenberg, of Germany, about 1450. Before this time, all books and papers were either hand-written or printed from engraved wooden blocks. To-day there are over 50,000 faces and sizes of type. Type is divided into three great classes: (1) Roman or body type, which is used for the reading matter in newspapers, magazines, and books; (2) display type, which appears in headings, and is used for circulars and the like; and (3) ornamental type, which has a fancy face. The different sizes of type formerly bore arbitrary names, like Nonpareil, Pica, etc., but now all type is under the point system, Nonpareil being known as 6 Point and Pica as 12 Point. The reading matter in all large daily newspapers is set in 6 Point, but most books are printed from either 10, 11, or 12 Point. Twelve Point type has twice the depth of 6 Point type. Type to be set is placed in two cases, one known as upper case and the other as lower case, the former holding capitals and small capitals; the latter small letters and figures, both cases containing boxes for spaces and other characters. The compositor holds in his left hand what is known as a composing stick, or stick. It is made of metal, with a bottom and three sides, the left side being movable and adjustable.

The compositor places one piece of type at a time in the stick, setting the type from left to right and upside down. He places metal spaces between each word. When a line is completed, he sets another, with or without a piece of thin metal between the lines, known as a lead. When the stick is full, he dumps his type into a galley, which is a receptacle made of wood or metal, from one to three feet long, framed at the bottom and at the sides, but open at the other end. The type is then locked up in a steel frame or chase, and is ready to be stereotyped, electrotyped, or to be printed from.

United States Flag.—On June 14, 1777, the United States Congress declared " that the flag of the thirteen United States be thirteen stripes, alternate red and white; that the Union be thirteen stars, white in a blue field, representing the new constellation." In 1794 Congress decreed that after May 1st, 1795, " The flag of the United States be fifteen stripes, alternate red and white, and that the Union be fifteen stars, white in a blue field." At that time the stars and stripes were of equal number, and it was the intention to add both a star and stripe with the addition of each new State. Subsequently, it was found that the addition of a stripe for each new State would produce a flag altogether too large. Accordingly, Congress, on April 4th, 1818, reduced the number of stripes to thirteen and made the number of stars twenty, that being the number of States at that time. It was further enacted that a new star should be added as each new State was admitted into the Union. By act of Congress, the flag has become a sacred emblem, and cannot be used for other than decorative or patriotic purposes, and cannot serve as a part of an advertisement or other announcement.

United States History in Brief

1492, August 3, Columbus sailed from Palos, Spain.

1492, October 12, Columbus discovered America.

1607, May 13, the English made first permanent settlement at Jamestown, Virginia.

1609, September 11, Henry Hudson, commanding the " Half Moon," sailed into New York Harbor.

1620, November 11, the " Mayflower," containing the Pilgrims, arrived at Provincetown, Massachusetts.

1620, December 22, the " Mayflower " landed at Plymouth Rock, Plymouth, Massachusetts.

1690, September 25, the first American newspaper was published at Boston, Massachusetts.

1732, February 22, George Washington, first President of the Republic, was born.

1743, April 13, Thomas Jefferson was born.

1765, March 22, Passage of the Stamp Act.

1767, March 15, Andrew Jackson born.

1770, March 5, massacre and riot in the streets of Boston, Massachusetts.

1773, December 16, the famous Boston Tea party was organized.

1775, April 18, the ride of Paul Revere, warning inhabitants of the coming battles of Lexington and Concord, Massachusetts.

1775, April 19, the battle of Lexington and Concord, Massachusetts.

1775, May 20, the first Declaration of Independence was signed at Mecklenburg, North Carolina.

1775, June 17, Battle of Bunker Hill, at Charlestown, Massachusetts.

1776, March 17, the British evacuated Boston.

1776, June 17, George Washington was appointed Commander-in-Chief of the American forces.

1776, July 4, The Declaration of Independence was formally signed at Philadelphia.

1776, August 27, Battle of Long Island.

1776, December 26, Battle of Trenton.

1781, October 19, Cornwallis surrendered his army, at Yorktown, Virginia.

1783, January 20, the United States and Great Britain agreed upon secession of hostilities.

1783, November 25, New York was evacuated by the British.

1789, April 30, George Washington was inaugurated first President of the United States.

1790, June 28, Washington, District of Columbia, was made the Capital of the United States.

1791, August 30, Issue of the first United States patent.

1792, April 2, United States Mint established at Philadelphia, Pennsylvania.

1793, September 18, Laying of the corner stone of the capitol, at Washington, District of Columbia.

1784, May 8, Congress established the Post-Office Department.

1796, September 17, President Washington issued his Farewell Address.

1799, December 14, death of President Washington.

1807, January 19, birth of General Robert E. Lee.

1807, August 11, first trial trip of a steamboat, by Robert Fulton, its inventor, on the Hudson River.

1809, February 12, birth of Abraham Lincoln.

1813, September 10, Perry's victory on Lake Erie.

1815, January 8, Battle of New Orleans.

1816, December 13, establishment, at Boston, Massachusetts, of the first Savings Bank in the United States.

1819, May 22, the first steam vessel to cross

the Atlantic Ocean sailed from Atlanta, Georgia.

1844, May 27, first telegraph message sent by Professor Morse, the inventor of telegraphy.

1846, April 23, beginning of the Mexican War.

1847, February 22, Battle of Buena Vista.

1847, September 14, capture of the city of Mexico by the United States Army.

1851, August 27, the Yacht "America" won the international cup race, at Cowes, England.

1858, August 16, the Old World and the New World connected by telegraphic cable.

1859, October 18, capture of John Brown, at Harper's Ferry, Virginia.

1860, December 20, South Carolina seceded from the Union.

1861, April 12, Fort Sumter, South Carolina, bombarded.

1861, April 15, President Lincoln issued his first call for volunteers.

1861, July 21, Battle of Bull Run.

1862, March 9, Fight in Hampton Roads, Virginia, between the "Monitor" and the "Merrimac."

1862, April 28, New Orleans evacuated.

1862, June 6, capture of Memphis, Tennessee.

1862, September 15, General Stonewall Jackson captured Harper's Ferry.

1862, September 17, Battle of Antietam.

1863, January 1, President Lincoln issued the Proclamation of Emancipation.

1863, February 25, passage of the National Bank Act.

1863, July 1 to 3, Battle of Gettysburg.

1863, September 19, Battle of Chickmauga.

1864, March 6 to 8, Battle of the Wilderness.

1864, June 19, the Warship "Kearsarge" sank the "Alabama."

1864, September 2, General Sherman captured Atlanta, Georgia.

1865, April 9, General Lee surrendered at Appomattox.

1865, April 14, John Wilkes Booth assassinated President Lincoln.

1867, March 30, Treaty for the purchase of Alaska signed.

1869, May 10, completion of the Union Pacific Railroad.

1871, October 8, great fire at Chicago.

1881, July 2, President Garfield shot by Charles J. Guiteau.

1886, May 4, Haymarket riot at Chicago.

1889, May 31, great flood at Johnstown, Pennsylvania.

1893, February 14, the Hawaiian Islands annexed to the United States.

1897, June 14, Venezuela boundary line treaty ratified by Congress.

1898, February 15, United States Battleship "Maine" blown up in Havana Harbor.

1898, April 21, Severance of diplomatic relations between Spain and the United States.

1898, April 27, Matanzas, Cuba, fired upon by American warships.

1898, May 1, Admiral Dewey destroyed the Spanish fleet at Manila.

1898, May 6, United States fleet bombarded Santiago, Cuba.

1898, May 12, Admiral Sampson fired upon San Juan, Porto Rico.

1898, June 3, Hobson sank the Merrimac in the harbor of Santiago. that he might block the channel.

1898, June 22, first landing of the United States troops in Cuba.

1898, July 3, the Spanish fleet destroyed at Santiago.

1898, July 16, Santiago surrendered.

1898, August 13, Manila surrendered.

1898, November 28, end of the Spanish-American War.

1901, September 6, President McKinley killed by Leon Czolgolz.

1901, September 16, Hay-Pauncefote Canal Treaty ratified by Congress.

1902, July 4, Declaration of Peace with Philippine Islands, and amnesty granted to all insurgents.

1904, May 4, the United States took control of the Panama Canal.

1909, April 6, R. E. Peary discovered North Pole.

1911, January 3, Postal Banks established in United States.

1914, August 2, Germany invades Belgium.

1914, August 15, Panama Canal opened.

1915, May 7, "Lusitania" sunk.

1917, April 6, United States declared state of war existed with Germany; December 7, with Austria.

1918, November 11, Armistice in World War signed.

1919, June 28, Peace Treaty signed between Allies and Germany.

1920, January 16, Eighteenth Amendment proclaimed in effect.

1920, August 26, Nineteenth Amendment proclaimed in effect.

1921, July 2, United States Peace Treaty with Germany and Austria signed.

1921, Nov. 12, President Harding opens Disarmament Conference.

Utopia.—An imaginary island, the inhabitants of which enjoy perfect laws and institutions. It is described in Sir Thomas More's political romance, "De Optimo Reipublicae Statu, deque Nova Insula Utopia."

Vaccination.—Vaccination, a preventive of smallpox, was discovered by Dr. Edward Jenner, of England. It consists of injecting into the blood a virus made from the sores or scabs of cows suffering from cowpox, or the virus may be taken from the sore coming from vaccination itself. Comparatively few people, properly vaccinated, can have the smallpox, and are largely exempt from any disease resembling it, except that which is known as varioloid, which is a mild form of smallpox. It is not known how long vaccination remains a preventive, but probably for seven years, when one should be vaccinated again. The prejudice against vaccination, which was very intense at its discovery, no longer exists except among a few. Practically every physician advocates it, and it is compulsory in some towns and cities. Deaths have occurred from it, but they are very infrequent.

Vacuum.—The perfect vacuum, which it is impossible to produce, is space without air or atmosphere. Vacuums are made by pumping all the air out of a receptacle or chamber. In a vacuum, everything falls at the same rapidity, as there is nothing to buoy it up, a feather descending as rapidly as lead shot.

Vedas.—Sacred writings of the Hindus, hymns, prayers, and liturgies, said to have been compiled by Vyasa about 1200 B. C. They are written in Sanskrit, and divided into four parts.

Voodooism.—A degraded form of religion prevalent among the negroes of Hayti and the Southern States of America. Supposed to be a relic of the religion of equatorial Africa.

Watered Stock.—It is said that the late Commodore Vanderbilt originated what is known as watered stock. Watered stock is capitalizing an industry at a figure in advance of its real value. For example: a railroad has tangible assets of $10,000,000, and an earning capacity sufficient to pay a 6 per cent. dividend on its capitalization; financial giants manipulate the stock and increase it to, say, $20,000,000, watering it to the extent of 100 per cent. In other words, the real value of the stock then is one-half of what it was in the first place. Stock watering has become epidemic, and is the cause of hundreds of thousands of financial failures. The stock waterers, however, as a rule, win, the public being the victims.

Wealth of the Nations.—The estimated wealth of the principal nations of the earth is given in billions: United States, 204; Great Britain and Ireland, 70; France, 58; Germany 80; Russia, 58; Italy, 21; Belgium, 5.8; Spain, 1.4; Netherlands, 5; Portugal, 2.5; Switzerland, 3.8.

Weather Flags

The Weather Bureau maintained by the United States Department of Agriculture displays at its stations flags which indicate probable changes in the weather.

A white flag indicates clear or fair weather.

A blue flag, rain or snow.

A flag with the upper half white and the lower half blue, local rain or snow.

A black triangular flag indicates temperature.

A white flag with black square in center, a cold wave.

When the black triangular flag is placed above the white flag, the black flag or the white and blue flag, it indicates warmer weather; when below, colder.

When the black triangular flag is not displayed at all, the temperature is likely to remain stationary.

Flags are displayed by the Weather Bureau as storm warnings in the following manner:

Small Craft Warning: A red pennant indicates that moderately strong winds are expected.

Storm Warning: A red flag with a black center indicates that a storm of marked violence is expected.

The pennants displayed with the flags indicate the direction of the wind—white, westerly (from southwest to north); red, easterly (from northeast to south). The pennant above the flag indicates that the wind is expected to blow from the northerly quadrants; below, from the southerly quadrants.

By night a red light indicates easterly winds, and a white light below a red light, westerly winds.

Hurricane Warning: Two red flags with

black centers, displayed one above the other, indicate the expected approach of a tropical hurricane, or one of those extremely severe and dangerous storms which occasionally move across the Lakes and Northern Atlantic coast.

No night small craft or hurricane warnings are displayed.

Wedding. Anniversaries.—First, cotton; Second, paper; Third, leather; Fourth, fruit and flowers; Fifth, wooden; Sixth, sugar; Seventh, woolen; Eighth, India rubber; Ninth, willow; Tenth, tin; Eleventh, steel; Twelfth, silk and fine linen; Thirteenth, lace; Fourteenth, ivory; Fifteenth, crystal; Twentieth, china; Twenty-fifth, silver; Thirtieth, pearl; Fortieth, ruby; Fiftieth, golden; Seventy-fifth, diamond.

Weights and Measures
LONG MEASURE

12 inches	1 foot
3 feet	1 yard
2 yards	1 fathom
16½ feet	1 rod
4 rods	1 chain
10 chains	1 furlong
8 furlongs	1 mile
3 miles	1 league

SQUARE MEASURE

9 square feet	1 square yard
30¼ square yards	1 square rod
40 square rods	1 rood

4 roods...1 acre
640 acres......................................1 square mile
    An acre is 43,560 square feet.

DRY MEASURE

2 pints...1 quart
8 quarts...1 peck
4 pecks..1 bushel

LIQUID MEASURE

4 gills..1 pint
2 pints...1 quart
4 quarts...1 gallon

TROY WEIGHT

24 grains.................................1 pennyweight
20 pennyweights............................1 ounce
12 ounces....................................1 pound

AVOIRDUPOIS WEIGHT

16 drams.....................................1 ounce
16 ounces....................................1 pound
25 pounds...................................1 quarter
4 quarters.................................1 hundred
20 hundreds.................................1 ton

APOTHECARIES' WEIGHT

20 grains....................................1 scruple
3 scruples....................................1 dram
8 drams......................................1 ounce
12 ounces....................................1 pound

CUBIC MEASURE

1728 cubic inches.....................1 cubic foot
27 cubic feet.........................1 cubic yard
16 cubic feet.........................1 cord foot
8 cord feet.............................. 1 cord
128 cubic feet........................1 cord

LAND MEASURE

```
7.92 inches.....................................1 link
25 links........................................1 rod
4 rods.........................................1 chain
80 chains......................................1 mile
```

CIRCULAR MEASURE

```
60 seconds.....................................1 minute
60 minutes.....................................1 degree
30 degrees.....................................1 sign
60 degrees.....................................1 sextant
90 degrees.....................................1 quadrant
360 degrees....................................1 circle
```

METRIC SYSTEM

MEASURES OF WEIGHT
(Unit Gramme)

	Grains	Oz. Troy	Lbs. Avoir.	Cwt.
Centigramme	0.15432	.....	.....	.....
Decigramme	1.54323	0.003	.....	.....
Gramme	15.43235	0.032	0.002	.....
Decagramme	154.32349	0.321	0.022	.....
Hectogramme	1543.23488	3.215	0.220	0.001
Kilogramme 15432.34880		32.150	2.204	0.019

MEASURES OF LENGTH
(Unit Metre)

	Inches	Feet	Yards	Miles
Millimetre	0.03937	0.003	0.001	.....
Centimetre	0.3937I	0.032	0.010	.....
Decametre	393.70790	32.808	10.936	0.006
Metre	39.37079	3.280	1.093	.....
Decimetre	3.93708	0.328	0.109	.....
Hectometre	3937.07900	328.089	109.363	0.062
Kilometre 39370.79000		3280.899	1093.633	0.621

BOARD AND TIMBER MEASURE

BOARD MEASURE

In board measure boards are assumed to be one inch in thickness.

To compute the measure of surface in square feet—

When all dimensions are in feet, multiply the length by the breadth, and the product will give the surface required.

When either of the dimensions are in inches, multiply as above and divide by 12.

When all dimensions are in inches, multiply as before and divide product by 144.

TIMBER MEASURE

To compute the volume of round timber—

When all dimensions are in feet, multiply the length by the square of one-quarter of the main girt, and the product will give the measurement in cubic feet.

When length is given in feet and girt in inches, multiply as before and divide by 144.

When all the dimensions are in inches, multiply as before and divide by 1,728.

Sawed or hewed timber is measured by the cubic foot. To compute the volume of square timber—

When all dimensions are in feet, multiply the product of the breadth by the depth by the length, and the product will give the volume in cubic feet.

When either of the dimensions are in inches, multiply as above and divide the product by 12.

When any two of the dimensions are in inches, multiply as before and divide the product by 144.

WHAT TO DO IN EMERGENCIES

Many books and pamphlets have been written advising the layman what to do in a case of emergency, and in the absence of a physician or surgeon.

Much of the information presented is altogether too technical, and is not likely to be understood by the public at large.

The author has attempted to cover, in a few pages, the fundamentals of first aid to the injured, and has carefully avoided technical and medicinal terms. No amount of information, no matter how carefully or plainly written, can take the place of the physician or surgeon. Self-doctoring and -dosing is, or should be, considered a crime, and no one is justified in attempting to relieve any one suffering from accident or any other ailment, if it is of possible seriousness, unless a good physician or surgeon cannot be procured.

First and always, keep your head, and keep cool. Don't get excited. Work rapidly, but deliberately. If the injury or trouble is at all serious, summon a surgeon or physician immediately. If you are alone with the sufferer, it may not be safe for you to leave him, but unless he is in immediate danger, it is better to call a competent physician, even though you have to absent yourself from him for a few moments. If the accident occurs in a crowd, solicit some one who looks trustworthy, and request him to telephone or otherwise communicate with a doctor.

If you know the cause of the accident or trouble inform the physician in advance, so that he may be better prepared to meet it and bring with him instruments and remedies.

The patient or sufferer should be placed in

a comfortable position, a doctor or surgeon summoned, and in the interval the layman may follow the instructions presented here. If he does so, no harm will be done, and in many cases suffering will be relieved, and death or serious illness prevented. But the author again, and most emphatically, urges the layman to send for a physician or surgeon, and to follow the instructions or information given in this chapter only as preliminary to the arrival of the doctor or surgeon, unless the injury be of slight consequence.

If possible, remove the patient to a quiet place, where there is plenty of air, and where the temperature is normal.

If there are many people about, request them to keep away.

Place the injured person in a comfortable position, usually upon his back, and straighten out his legs and arms. If the head is injured, better lift it above the level of the body; but if it is not, allow the body to lie on a level.

If the patient is breathing hard, it may be well to lift him into a sitting position. Loosen his collar, waist-band, and clothing. If he faints, his head should be slightly lower than his feet. If an arm or leg is injured, lift it slightly and place it upon a cushion, pillow, or other support.

If the one injured is unconscious, watch him very carefully. If he is vomiting, or that tendency is apparent, turn him over on one

side so that the discharge will run out easily
and not go into the lungs.

If he is wounded, cut away the clothing
covering the wound, but don't remove any
more than is necessary. If he has been
burned, pour lukewarm water, containing a
little saleratus or bicarbonate of soda, over
the clothing before you remove it. If he is
bleeding severely, stop the bleeding before
dressing the wound. After the wound is
dressed there is nothing for the novice to do,
except bring the patient to consciousness, if
unconscious, and remove him to a place of
safety and comfort.

If the accident or injury be serious, or the
patient is unconscious, it is well to request
more than one bystander to summon a physician, because the first one sent may fail, or
the physician he telephones to or calls upon
may be unavailable.

Use the telephone, if there is one at hand
or nearby, and tell the physician what you
think is the matter with the sufferer or what
caused the accident, that he may be better
prepared to bring with him the instruments
necessary.

If you are alone with the patient, and cannot notify a physician or surgeon without
leaving the patient, you must use your best
judgment; but you should make every possible effort to reach a physician at the earliest
possible moment. Remain with the patient

long enough to place him in a comfortable position, and to stop the flow of blood, if bleeding; then make all haste to notify a physician or surgeon.

The author acknowledges his indebtedness to Johnson's First Aid Manual, published by Johnson & Johnson of New Brunswick, N. J., and to Jay W. Seaver, M. D., of New Haven, Conn., and recently of Yale University.

Accidents.—Convey the sufferer to a place of safety, and give him plenty of air. If a shock follows, follow instructions given for shock. Do not touch the wound with the bare hand. Wear absolutely clean gloves or wrap the fingers in clean cloth or gauze. Do not attempt to cleanse the wound. Summon a surgeon immediately.

Apparent Death.—Never assume that a person is dead because he appears to be. Summon a physician. A fairly good test of death is to hold the hand of the person apparently dead before a candle or other light, with the fingers stretched out, each touching the other. Gaze intently between the fingers, and if the person is alive, a red or pink color will undoubtedly be seen where the fingers touch each other. Another method is to take a cold piece of polished steel, like a razor blade or table knife, and hold before the mouth or nose of the person apparently dead. If moisture does not gather on it, it may be safe to assume that breathing has stopped; but these tests are not infallible.

Bandaging.—There are two kinds of bandages,—the roller bandage or the triangular or handkerchief bandage. They may be purchased at any drug store or be made on the spot in an emergency. The purchased bandages are made of gauze, or muslin, crinolin, elastic webbing, rubber, or other material. The roller bandages are absorbent, and are very thin and pliable. They should be placed next to the wound and hold the fluids. Muslin bandages are stronger than those made of gauze, and should be used for pressure and outside bandages. Bandages should be kept in a perfectly clean place, and always covered, either by being enclosed in a box or wrapped in paper. If an improvised bandage is used, care should be taken to use a clean cloth. The triangular bandage is made by cutting a piece of cloth about 36 inches square into two pieces diagonally. It can be purchased at a drug store, or any clean cloth can be used if it is of firm texture.

Baths.—Cold baths may be taken to reduce fever and in sunstroke and other cases when the temperature is high. It is well to have the temperature in the bath at 70° or 80° Fahrenheit, and to reduce the water until it reaches 60° or 65°. Tepid baths have a temperature of 80° or 90°, and warm baths are of a temperature from 90° to a little less than

100°. Hot baths may be used in case of shock, apparent drowning, depression, and similar troubles. The temperature of the water should vary from 98° to 110°. When the patient leaves the bath, he should be dried quickly and put to bed. Hot baths may produce fainting, and should be taken in the presence of an attendant. Do not guess at the temperature of the water; use a thermometer.

Bleeding.—Arterial blood, or blood coming from the arteries, is bright red, and is discharged in spurts or jets. Such bleeding is very dangerous, and unless a physician arrives almost immediately the patient is not likely to survive.

Venous blood, which comes from the veins, is of dark purple color and flows freely and steadily.

Capillary bleeding comes from injured small veins. It flows slowly, and such bleeding is dangerous only if it continues. Always summon a surgeon or physician, and put in a hurry call for him. Force the patient to lie down in a level position, preferably upon his back.

If the leg or arm is wounded, elevate it. Cut away the clothing quickly, so that it may be exposed. Press the bleeding places, but cover your finger with gauze or a clean handkerchief, or compress the part by using a strong cloth bandage.

If the bleeding comes from an artery, cover your finger with a few thicknesses of gauze or clean cloth, and press hard upon the wound and maintain the pressure, which may stop the bleeding. If the wound is large, crowd a lot of gauze into it, and push it in, then press on the flesh a little distance above the wound, that is, between the wound and the heart. This can be done by winding a bandage, a piece of rubber tubing, string, or rope, or a pair of suspenders may be used, above the wound.

If the arm or leg is crushed, do not press on the wound, but bring pressure to bear above it.

Bleeding from the Veins.—Lay a piece of gauze over the wound and bind it on with a firm bandage. Be very careful not to apply your naked fingers or hand to the wound unless you have washed them in some antiseptic, but even then it is better to cover your fingers with clean gauze or cloth. If the bleeding is very severe, apply cracked ice wrapped in gauze, and hard pressure below the wound. Varicose veins occasionally bleed. Elevate the arm or leg and bandage it very tightly, the bandage to be placed directly over the bleeding spot.

Bleeding from Capillary Veins.—As the blood oozes, and does not flow rapidly, expose the wound to the air for a short time, which will usually check it. The application of hot water is advisable, but warm water should not be used. Extremely cold water or cracked ice will stop some bleeding. If copious bleeding occurs around a tooth, it may be stopped by packing the place with plaster of Paris, or absorbent cotton may be used. In every case, keep the places warm. After the bleeding is stopped, give hot drinks, like hot tea, coffee, or milk, if much blood has been lost.

Broken Bones.—Do not attempt to set the break. Handle the patient carefully. Place him in a comfortable position and undress him, removing the clothing by cutting it to save time. If it is necessary to carry him a distance, improvise a splint made of wood or heavy pasteboard and fasten it around the broken part with bandages. Carry him to a physician or summon one at once, but let him lie quietly if a physician can reach him. It is well to have two splints, one on each side, to be held in place by the same bandages. If the arm is broken, bandage it and place it in a sling. In every case, summon a physician or carry the patient to one.

Chilblains.—Keep the feet warm and dry. Don't warm them at a fire or place them in hot water, but bathe them in cold water and rub with a dry towel. Apply turpentine, camphorated spirits, or oil of wintergreen.

Cleanliness

It is said that cleanliness is next to godliness. Good health is dependent upon the care of the body, and the body will not remain in a healthful state unless frequently bathed.

The fact that thousands of persons enjoy good health without even taking an infrequent bath, must not be used as an argument against regular bathing. These persons, if in health, live out of doors, and Nature seems to take care of them; but it is obvious that they would be healthier and stronger if they gave proper attention to bodily cleanliness.

The majority of city dwellers, and a large proportion of those living in the country, work indoors, and their health is dependent upon their personal cleanliness.

Opinions differ, and some hygienists do not consider the daily bath essential, but the majority of those who have studied the subject maintain that perfect health requires the daily bathing of the entire body.

Without the daily bath one does not begin his work refreshed or with exhilaration.

A scrub is not to be recommended more than once a week, but a bath should be taken daily, and the entire body rubbed with a dry towel, a bath towel to be preferred. Emersion in a tub of water is not necessary, although it is the best and easiest way of taking a bath, next to a shower bath. A sponge bath answers all purposes.

A cold plunge should not be taken without the advice of a physician. The shower bath is very refreshing. A hot bath is seldom advisable. It is better to have the water of a temperature not much higher than that of summer heat. A pure soap should be used, and care should be taken to rinse it from the body. The daily bath is the best preventive of colds. Comparatively few people who bathe daily suffer from more than transient colds.

The bath should not be taken in a draught. If the room is cold, work rapidly and use additional time for rubbing, continuing it until the skin glows.

The practice of partial bathing is not to be recommended. When you take a bath, take it all over.

If away from home, and sleeping in a hotel bed, which may have been occupied by a diseased person, it is well to go over the body carefully in the morning with an antiseptic soap. Every hotel, and all public conveyances, are laden with germs, and a bath will prevent many diseases.

A few drops of ammonia or a teaspoonful of borax placed in the water in which you bathe will remove the odor of perspiration, but ammonia should not take the place of good soap.

Clothing Afire.—Force the person afire to lie down and roll him over and over. Wrap him in a rug or blanket, or anything else at hand. Throw water upon him, but do not wait for water. Wrapping him in a blanket is sure to extinguish the flames. Under no circumstances allow the person afire to run about or out of doors.

Colds.—Use simple remedies, such as hot lemonade, but if the cold does not soon abate, consult a physician.

Diphtheria. — Consult your physician. Never go near a case of diphtheria or allow a dog, cat, or other animal to enter the sickroom. Be careful of every utensil, and do not allow any one else to use them until they have been washed in antiseptics. Never handle any clothing or other articles in a sickroom.

Disinfectants

The reader is warned against placing reliance upon any disinfectant, because it smells of carbolic acid, or has any other strong odor. Many of the advertised disinfectants are worthless, and some of them are merely deodorizers, which destroy smell and don't disinfect.

Sulphur or brimstone is probably the best fumigator. Sulphite of iron (copperas) is cheap and should be used for sewers and drains. Dissolve a pound and a half in a gallon of water. Two parts of sulphate of zinc to one part of common salt, dissolved in a gallon of water, is a good disinfectant for clothing, bed linen, etc.

Carbolic acid is an excellent disinfectant, but is efficacious only when used at considerable strength, 3 to 5 per cent. Its strong odor suggests qualities which do not exist, if it is much diluted.

There are many disinfectants upon the market, many of them being advertised to be efficacious. Some of them are thoroughly reliable, but others are almost worthless. I would advise the reader not to purchase or use a disinfectant which is not recommended by a reliable physician.

Disinfecting Cellars, Yards, Cesspools, etc. —Use a solution made of 60 pounds of copperas dissolved in a barrel of water. Sprinkle freely over cellar and put a pailful in a cesspool.

Disinfecting the Sick-Room.—Plenty of fresh air and cleanliness are to be first considered. The clothing, bed linen, and towels should be washed in a tub containing a zinc chloride solution, and the water should be boiling hot. A solution of copperas and water should be immediately placed in all vessels containing discharges.

Dislocations.—The novice should never attempt to treat a dislocation. All he can do is to place the patient in a comfortable position, using a sling or cushion to support the part injured. A physician should be summoned.

Dog Bites.—Wash the wound with antiseptic soap or pure soap and water, with borax dissolved in it to the strength of a teaspoonful to a pint. Hydrophobia occurs very infrequently, and many dogs, supposed to be mad, are suffering from some other ailment; but a surgeon should be summoned in all cases whenever it is possible to do so. The bite of a rat, cat, or other animal is not generally dangerous, but the wound should be washed with borax and water, as above. Better summon a surgeon. Suck the wound vigorously before applying washes. There is no danger to the person sucking a wound of this nature, unless the skin on his lips or in his mouth is cracked or bleeding, but he may wash his mouth with borax water if he feels uneasy about it.

Drowning

If the person is conscious tell him that you will save him, which will prevent him from losing his nerve. If you swim out for him, and he is struggling, seize him by the hair and turn him over on his back. Swim on your side, towing him along as you would a log of wood. You may hold his head with one arm, but do not attempt to support his entire body. If he struggles violently, hold his head under water until he is unconscious, so that you can better handle him. Loosen his clothing, drain water out of lungs by inverting body, clean out his mouth, and pull his tongue forward. Immediately begin artificial respiration, each movement to last from four to five seconds. Apply warmth and rubbing, and when he is conscious give him hot water, coffee, or lemonade. Artificial breathing is of greatest consequence. Do not give up. Many persons have been resuscitated after many hours of incessant labor. Artificial respiration may be performed in the following way:

First—Immediately loosen the clothing about the neck and chest, exposing them to the wind, except in very severe weather. Get the water out of the body, first by tickling throat with a feather, or applying ammonia to the nose; give a severe slap with the open hand upon the chest and soles of feet; if no immediate result, proceed as follows:

Second—Lay the body down in the open air with the head hanging down and with its weight on the stomach across any convenient object, such as a keg, box, boat timber, or your knees. Open the mouth quickly, drawing the tongue forward with handkerchief or cloth to let the water escape. Keep the mouth clear of liquid. To relieve the pressure on the stomach, roll the body gently from side to side and then back on the stomach. Do this several times to force the water from the stomach and throat.

Third—Lay the body on the back, make a

roll of a coat or any garment, place it under the shoulders of the patient, allowing the head to fall back. Then kneel at the head of the patient.

Open patient's mouth and place some small object between teeth.

With tongue pliers or fingers covered with gauze or cloth, grasp his tongue and draw it out. Tie it down to his chin with cloth or rubber band.

Grasp the patient's arms at the middle of the forearms, fold them across his stomach, and raise them over his head to a perpendicular position, drawing them backward, straight, then forward overhead to the sides again, pressing the arms on the lower part of the ribs and side, so as to produce a bellows movement upon the lungs. Do this about fifteen times a minute.

Apply smelling salts, camphor, or ammonia to the nostrils to excite breathing.

Fourth—On signs of life, or when breathing is restored, remove the clothing, dry the body, wrap the patient in warm blankets or hot cloths. To encourage circulation briskly rub his limbs under the blankets toward the heart; brandy or aromatic spirits of ammonia may be given in small doses, with care to avoid strangulation.

Another Method

Another simple method of restoring breathing, one that is being rapidly adopted, is that known as the Schafer, or prone, method. It has the great advantage that it can be performed by one man alone. This method has just been endorsed as the preferable one by a commission representing the American Medical Association, the National Electric Light Association, and the American Institute of Electrical Engineers.

First—Lay patient on stomach with his head to side and withdraw his tongue, which itself then will hang out if teeth are held apart with small object. The operator then kneels astride the patient's thighs and with his hands across the lower ribs swings his body back and forth rhythmically, pausing about two seconds as his weight falls upon and is removed from patient. This movement is to be continued at the rate of about fifteen times a minute.

To Prevent Drowning.—The human body weighs, in the water, about one pound; that is, it is approximately one pound heavier than the water which it displaces. A stool, chair, or small box or board will overcome the tendency to sink and will keep the head above water. The feet, and the hand which is not clinging to an object, should be used as paddles. Every one should learn to swim. If he can take only a few strokes, the chances of death by drowning are small, for he is likely to be able to reach something which will support him. So much do I believe in the necessity of knowing how to swim, that I consider it a crime not to understand this art.

Electrical Accidents.—Immediately shut off the current, but do not handle the wire with your naked hands. If rubber gloves are not handy, cut the wire with an ax or knife, with a piece of woolen cloth wrapped around the handle. If you pull the sufferer away from the wire, do not touch him with your bare hands, but cover them with woolen cloth, or wear rubber or woolen gloves, or remove him by the use of a rope. The ordinary electric shock will not cause death unless the patient continues to receive it. Summon a doctor at once. Place the patient in the open air, with something under his shoulders. Loosen his clothing, open his mouth, and pull out the tongue. Clear the mouth from saliva. Force air into his lungs by pressing the base of the ribs about once in four seconds, then attempt to resuscitate him as you would a drowning person.

Emergencies with Children.—If the child suddenly suffers from vomiting, purging, and prostration, send for a doctor at once. In the meantime place him in a hot bath and then carefully dry him with a warm towel and wrap in warm blankets. If the hands and feet are cold, apply hot water bottles to the feet and hands. A poultice made of flaxseed meal

(¾) and mustard (¼) should be placed over
the body. Five drops of brandy in a teaspoonful of water may be given every 15
minutes. For sudden diarrhœa, administer one
teaspoonful of castor oil or of spiced syrup of
rhubarb. Allow the child to drink freely of
cold water that has been boiled. Always
summon a physician.

Emergency Medicines ..

The writer would emphatically discourage
self-medication and dosing, and would oppose
the taking of medicines of any kind, except
the simplest remedies, without the advice of
a physician. Hundreds of thousands of people have been made sick, because the wrong
medicine was administered to them, and
many more have taken medicine when they
didn't need it.

The following emergency medicines are
presented, with a distinct understanding that
they should not be used except in simple
cases:

Ammonia.—What is known as ammonia
water, or liquor of ammonia, or as spirits of
hartshorn, or hartshorn, is of several strengths
and is highly irritating and poisonous if taken
internally. Applied externally, if of considerable strength, it will cause blisters and pain.
Ammonia should not be applied to an open
wound or irritated surface, except in case of
snake bites or stings of insects, where it is

intended to neutralize the poisons. The vapor of ammonia water, inhaled through the nostrils, affects the nervous system and may be used in fainting or epilepsy, but always with caution, for a strong preparation of ammonia applied to the nose may produce a violent shock. It is better to saturate a handkerchief or wad of cotton and hold it a short distance from the nostrils. The buyer is cautioned against the use of the strongest ammonia water.

Aromatic Spirits of Ammonia.—This is a stimulant, and may be used in cases of sick headache, hysteria, cholic, or fainting, in doses of from 10 to 30 drops in sweetened water.

Arnica.—Tincture of arnica is supposed to be of value in accidents, and especially efficacious for sprains and bruises. It has some value, mainly from the alcohol it contains and partly because it is applied with friction. It is a poison, and never should be taken internally. For external use it should not be applied at full strength, as it is apt to cause inflammation if the skin is tender.

Bicarbonate of Soda.—Bicarbonate of soda, commonly known as baking soda or saleratus, is distinct from sal soda or washing soda. It is of great value in the treatment of burns, and may be used as an antidote in poisoning by acids.

Camphor.—Camphor is purchased in gum or in liquid form. It never should be taken internally, except by advice of a physician. Nor should it be applied in its full strength directly to the wounds or to irritated or inflamed surfaces.

Ginger.—The essence or extract of ginger is a very popular remedy for trouble with the digestive organs, bowel complaints, etc., and should be taken in doses of from 10 to 40 drops in sweetened water, milk, or other liquid. It never should be used habitually, because it may establish a drug habit; nor should large doses be taken to check diarrhœa, as it is often inadvisable to too rapidly check the discharges.

Glycerin.—Glycerin may be used for burns, and, mixed with equal parts of rose water, it is a good lotion for chapped hands or lips, but it is irritating to the skin of some people.

Peppermint.—The essence of peppermint may be used for stomach-ache and bowel complaints, the usual dose being from 10 to 20 drops on sugar or in sweetened water. Oil of peppermint should not be taken, except when prescribed by a physician.

Turpentine.—Turpentine is the base of most liniments, and it has some value, but mustard plasters are safer. Turpentine is inflammable, and never should be applied near an open fire. Turpentine should not be given internally, unless prescribed by a physician.

Whisky.—Whisky, brandy, wine, and all other spirits should be used sparingly. They are likely to do more harm than good. Hot water, hot coffee, hot tea, or aromatic spirits of ammonia are to be preferred. Children should never be given spirituous liquids, except in extreme cases, and then only 10 to 20 drops in water.

Witch Hazel or Hamamelis.—Used as a remedy for sprains, wounds, and swelling. It is a mild application for chapped hands, and used by the laity for burns, scalds, cuts, etc. It is not irritating, and is a good substitute for arnica. Its use externally is absolutely safe.

Vaseline.—It is to be recommended for burns, scalds, etc. It is nonirritating and is not poisonous. It can be used frequently.

Cold Cream.—A perfectly safe article to be used for chapped hands and lips, and skin roughness.

Emetics and Stimulants.—In practically all cases, and where poison has entered the stomach, it is well to empty the stomach immediately. If a stomach pump cannot be procured, an emetic should be administered. Doctors would administer ipecac, apomorphine, sulphate of zinc, tartar emetic, and other drugs, but none of them are likely to be available before the physician arrives. When notifying the physician tell him, if possible, the kind of poison taken, so he may be prepared. A dessert-spoonful of ground dry mustard in a glass of warm water is likely to produce vomiting. Follow the first dose with a second one. Then push the forefinger down the throat as far as possible, that the patient may vomit. Dissolve a teaspoonful of salt in water and give to the patient, or administer a teaspoonful of ipecac every few minutes to a child, and a tablespoonful to an adult. Follow the dose with a glass of water and then insert the forefinger in the throat. One who has taken opium does not vomit easily and strenuous efforts should be made to produce vomiting. If one emetic does not work, give another, and keep on repeating it.

Exercise

Physical exercises are absolutely essential to health. The working man, however, is likely to obtain enough of it from his daily action, but those of sedentary habits, especially those who work indoors, will not receive sufficient exercise from their labor.

While the gymnasium is to be recommended, and while it has done much to make weak people strong, I would not advise any one to take more than very simple gymnasium exercises without the advice of a physician. Exercises may be taken in the bedroom, with the use of light dumb bells, or without the use of any apparatus at all.

Walking is the best of all, for it can be enjoyed by those in poor health or physically weak. It takes one out of doors, and exercise out of doors is far better than that taken in a closed room. If you exercise at home, open all of the windows.

Every one should walk at least two miles a day in the open air, unless he is very weak. Select a companion, as exercise is more efficacious if enjoyed and is not mere exercise by itself. Take long breaths in the open air every morning. Overexercise, and much of that practiced by athletes, injure the heart and work opposite from the intention. No strenuous exercise should be taken after mid-life without the advice of a physician. Any good doctor will prescribe a course of exercises for you at a nominal fee, most of them not charging more than a dollar for advice. Then, those who exercise need more food and a different kind of food from that required by those who do not exercise.

As cases differ, it is inadvisable for me to prescribe proper food. Consult your physician.

Extinguishing Fires from Coal Oil.—Do not attempt to smother the flame by water. Smother it with a carpet or cloth.

Fainting

Ordinary fainting is distinct from that which occurs from shock or collapse, the latter following serious injuries, while fainting is common with some people, and may not be serious.

Those who are subject to frequent fainting spells should consult a physician that he may locate the cause.

If fainting is caused from any disease of the heart, or from a weak heart, death may follow, and such persons should be under the care of a physician.

When fainting occurs, place the patient on his back with his head as low or lower than the body. Raise the legs. He should have plenty of fresh air. If fainting occurs in a crowd, ask the spectators to move away. If in-doors, open all doors and windows, loosen the clothing, and sprinkle water upon the face, at the same time applying smelling salts or spirits of camphor held close to the nose, but not touching it. The body may be rubbed to assist the circulation. If the person does not quickly revive, apply gentle heat or a mustard plaster to the pit of the stomach. When he recovers give him hot tea or coffee, and never more than a moderate amount of alcoholic stimulants. Keep him in a reclining position for some time after he has recovered.

Feeding an Invalid.—If the illness is at all

serious, consult a physician. He will tell you what and what not to give the patient in the way of food. Never cook the food in the presence of the invalid, and keep the smell of cooking away from him. Don't eat in his presence, as it may annoy him. Serve every-thing attractively, with spotless napkin, table cloth, and ware. Be careful not to spill any-thing. Hot articles should be served very hot, and cold ones very cold, as lukewarm viands are not acceptable. Everything brought into the sick-room should be covered with dishes or napkins. Better bring in too little than too much, more to be served if the patient desires it.

Fire in the House.—When the house is afire cover the head, if possible, with a wet cloth, or dry one if there is no facility for wetting it, cutting holes for the eyes. Creep on the floor and don't stand up or walk, for the air is clearer next to the floor, as smoke rises. Unless there are plenty of exits, a knotted rope should be attached to a staple. It is easier to climb down a knotted rope than one which is smooth. If necessary to jump from an upper story, throw out a mattress or some-thing else which is soft, and attempt to land upon it. When at a hotel or boarding house, ascertain the means of exit before retiring.

Fits.—Generally speaking, the treatment should be similar to that given to one who has fainted. If the patient is hysterical, apply mustard plasters or ice to the soles of his feet and the wrists, but do not dash water in the face or use strong emetics or heroic measures. If the fit is caused by epilepsy (in this case the person is rigid), do not attempt to stop the patient from struggling. Lay him on his back with his head somewhat raised, and loosen his clothing. If necessary, hold his arms and legs gently, but do not use force. Place a stick or knife handle between the teeth to prevent biting the tongue. Always summon a phyiscian.

Frost Bite.—Never place the patient near a fire. Undress him carefully and pack frozen parts with cloths wet with ice water. Rub adjacent parts vigorously. Administer hot coffee or tea. If breathing appears to have stopped, treat him as you would one apparently drowned. When the patient begins to revive, place him in a warm, but not a hot, room, cover him with blankets, and rub him with a cloth wrung out of hot water; give him the ordinary stimulants, but not alcoholic ones.

Fumigating a Sick-Room.—Formalin is probably the best fumigator. Place the articles to be fumigated in a closed room, and pour formaldehyde over towels or bed linen and place on the floor. The room should remain closed for 24 hours. A room containing

100 square feet of floor surface requires at least a pint of formaldehyde.

Getting Things into the Eye, Nose, Ear, etc.

Eye.—Sometimes complications result of a most serious nature. A physician should be sent for immediately. In the interval the following directions may be followed: Articles like cinders, dust, and other small objects may be removed from the eye, if one has a steady hand; but the eye should not be rubbed, and should be kept closed, except when one is trying to remove the foreign substance. The tears by themselves will often wash out ordinary dust or cinders. If the substance is hidden from view, one or two grains of whole flaxseed may remove it. Catch the upper lid by the lashes and pull away from the eyeball over the lower lid, holding it there for a moment, and request the patient to blow his nose vigorously. Visible articles may be removed with a piece of gauze on the hand, or an absolutely clean cloth; but don't touch the eye with the finger. As the eye is a very delicate organ, the novice should not attempt to operate upon it.

Nose.—Blow the nose very hard, and close one side of the nostril by pressing your finger against it. Tickle the nose or give snuff to excite sneezing. Sometimes the article will be removed if the patient takes a long breath and closes his mouth, then give him a sharp blow on the back. If the body is not discharged, call a physician.

Ear.—There is great danger in tampering with the ear. Never insert needles or pins in an attempt to remove foreign substances. Better send for a physician. If live insects enter the ear, pour a small quantity of sweet oil or glycerin into the ear and very gently syringe it with warm water.

Throat.—Send for a physician immediately, and tell him what you think the matter is, so he may bring the necessary instruments. If there is no difficulty in breathing, wait for the physician. Slap the person on the back when the body is bent forward with face downwards, which will cause him to cough. Elevate him so that his head is lower than his body and slap him on the back while in this position.

Getting Wet.—Many colds are contracted on account of exposure to rain and moisture. Unless able to change your clothes, keep moving. It is said that very few colds are contracted while one is exercising.

Headaches.—Under no circumstances take a headache powder, or any drug whatsoever, without the advice of your physician. Many headache powders contain dangerous drugs, which work upon the heart, sometimes causing death. Headaches almost invariably come from a cause not located in the head itself. Do not attempt to cure it yourself. The headache powder may relieve the headache temporarily at the expense of the system.

Hiccoughs.—Drink a glass full of cold water as rapidly as possible. Breathe deeply. If the hiccoughs continue, call a physician.

How to Avoid Accidents

Never cross the street without looking both ways.

Do not get off of a car or other vehicle while it is in motion.

Never thrust your head or arms out of the car or other vehicle.

When it is lightning, avoid trees and metallic articles.

Never allow firearms to be lying about. Have some one place for them and be sure that no one can get at them.

Move quickly when it is cold; and when any part is frozen, do not go near the fire, but rub with snow.

Always change wet clothing as soon as possible, and keep moving until you have opportunity to change.

Never walk on a railroad track.

Do not light a fire with kerosene or other inflammable fluid.

Never enter a cellar or anywhere else where gas is escaping with a light in your hand.

Under no circumstances touch a wire hanging in the street.

Maintain a medicine chest containing all of

the common remedies, but don't select them without the advice of your physician. Mark each bottle plainly, with directions under the label.

Never take medicine without looking at the label beforehand.

Illuminating Gas.—Summon a physician, and before he arrives proceed as follows: Remove the patient into fresh air and walk him around. Place his arms about your shoulders, and if there are two rescuers place one arm around the shoulders of each. A glass of Weiss beer should be given while the patient is walking, as it removes gas from the stomach. In five minutes give half a teaspoonful of aromatic spirits of ammonia in a third of a glass of water. Repeat this dose every 15 minutes until four doses have been given. The neck of the beer bottle may be forced into the patient's mouth.

Infectious Diseases.—It is now generally supposed that all contagious and communicable diseases are contracted by the germs which pass into the body or system. These germs are so small that millions of them may enter the body through the nose, throat, and skin. They do little or no harm to a healthy person, for the healthy body is opposed to their growth, but if one is weak, or suffering from a slight cold, or is depressed, they may multiply and cause diseases. These germs may be widely scattered,—in the clothes, bedding, carpets, and in the hair and skin. They cling to walls and ceilings and they will multiply on almost any kind of food. No one can wholly prevent coming into contact with them, but he can, if he will, avoid most of the contagious diseases by never sitting down in the sick-room, especially avoiding the bed, and keeping away from the walls and furniture. He should wash his hands with antiseptic soap after handling the patient. Exercise regularly in the open air. Nurses should wear washable dresses, which are frequently changed, and a washable cap should cover their hair. When in the sick-room do not approach the patient near enough to catch his breath. Do not touch with your lips any food, dish, or utensil which has been in the sick-room. Do not eat or drink in the sick-room. Wear no clothing that the patient wore before being taken sick. Never touch the sick person if your hands are sore or scratched, and be sure to wash them after contact with him. Never allow the dishes used by the patient to be used by any other unless they are very carefully washed and scalded in boiling water. All articles of food not eaten by the patient should be burned, and milk and food should never be allowed to stand in the sick-room. All bodily discharges should be immediately removed and covered with disinfecting solution, and the vessels should be washed with antiseptics before being brought back into the room.

Lockjaw.—Do not attempt to cure it. Consult your physician. It will probably be fatal.

Mustard Plasters.—Plasters occasionally are efficacious, but most give more apparent than real relief. They should not be used indiscriminately or without the advice of a physician.

Neuralgia.—This is often incurable, but may be relieved. Certain liniments are efficacious, but are not to be recommended indiscriminately. Better consult your physician.

Poison

Poisons taken into the system through the mouth, and not through the blood, require a different treatment.

Poisons may be classified as follows: 1. Irritant, in which the symptoms appear entirely at the location of the poison. 2. Systemic, in which the poison affects the system at large in addition to producing local irritation. 3. Narcotic or sleep-producing. 4. General, in which there is no local irritation.

In the first mentioned, it is best not to cause vomiting. Give dilute acids to neutralize alkalis, and dilute alkalis to neutralize acids. Then administer oil, raw egg, or flour and water. Small doses of opiates may be given to quiet the pain, and whisky or other spirituous liquor to relieve weakness.

In the second class (except for arsenic or similar poisoning) no emetic should be given. The poison may be counteracted by bland doses of oil, flour, and water, white of eggs; and stimulating drinks should be given to counteract depression.

In the third class, make strenuous effort to produce vomiting, then give strong coffee or other stimulating drinks, and make every effort to keep the patient awake, even if you have to keep him walking.

Fourth class. Give emetics, and follow with stimulating drinks to relieve weakness and pain. The patient should be allowed to rest.

Poisoning.

Poisoning by Acids.—For sulphuric, muriatic, nitric, and acetic acids give immediately a solution of baking soda or magnesia, chalk, lime, soap-suds, or chalk tooth powder, followed by raw eggs, milk, or sweet oil.

For Carbolic Acid or Creosote—Give alcohol and, immediately, castor oil, sweet oil, raw eggs, or milk, followed by an emetic.

For Oxalic Acid.—Administer lime, chalk, or magnesia. Lime may be scraped from the wall or ceiling and dissolved in water, but don't use soda, potash, or ammonia.

For Prussic Acid.—Generally the patient

dies immediately, but if he is still living, do not stop to give emetics, but administer stimulants. Apply hot and cold douches and use artificial respiration.

For Aconite Poisoning.—Wash the stomach with a stomach tube and avoid emetics. Use stimulants. Apply warmth to the extremities and place mustard plasters over the heart and legs. If the patient is insensible, use artificial respiration.

For Camphor.—Give emetics, oils, and eggs. Apply warmth to the extremities.

For Chloroform.—If caused by inhalation, resort to artificial respiration and apply friction. Place the patient in the fresh air, keeping the head very low. Alternate hot and cold applications. If it occurs from internal use, administer large doses of bicarbonate of soda in water. Administer artificial respiration if the patient is insensible.

For Nux Vomica.—Tobacco, chewing or smoking, and animal charcoal, dissolved in water. Follow with emetics. Use artificial respiration when necessary.

For Opium.—Administer an emetic, such as mustard or ipecac. Apply water to the head, face, and spine. Give strong coffee, but do not give alcoholic stimulants. Keep the patient aroused by walking, whipping, or other means. Use artificial respiration if necessary.

For Arsenic.—Give emetics immediately, including draughts of hot, greasy water or salt and water. Administer in large doses magnesia or lime scraped from the walls or ceilings. Give castor oil, sweet oil, or equal parts of sweet oil and lime water, or raw eggs. Use stimulants well diluted.

For Corrosive Sublimate.—Administer an emetic and large doses of white of eggs, milk, mucilage, barley water, or flour and water. Force the patient to swallow large quantities. Use the stomach pump.

For Belladonna.—Give emetics and stimulants. Apply warmth to extremities and mustard plasters to the feet. Use artificial respiration if necessary.

For Poisonous Mushrooms.—Give emetics, castor oil, stimulants, and apply heat.

Pulse.—The average rate of the pulse in adults is 76 beats every minute; but it varies according to age. At birth it is from 130 to 140; 1st year, 115 to 130; 2d year, 100 to 115; 3d year, 95 to 105; between 7 and 14, 80 to 90; between 14 and 21, 75 to 80; between 21 and 60, 70 to 75; in old age, from 75 to 80. The female pulse is from 10 to 15 beats quicker than that of the male of the same age. To count the pulse, place the finger over the artery at the wrist; count the beats for 15 seconds, multiply this by four, and the result is the number of beats a minute. Do not use the thumb, as there is a sort of pulse in it which interferes with counting.

Rheumatism.—So far as is known, there is no certain cure for rheumatism, notwithstanding the many nostrums that are advertised as sure cures. Rheumatism may be helped by avoiding meat and other nitrogenous foods, confining the diet to vegetables and similar foods, and drinking water freely. Rheumatism, however, is too serious to be treated by other than a physician.

Scalds and Burns

Place the patient in a comfortable and safe place and remove the clothing rapidly with a knife or scissors. If it sticks, cut away as much as is necessary, but don't pull it off. Clothing may sometimes be removed by sprinkling with water or oil. Do not expose the surface of the burn or scald to the air. Cover as quickly as possible with flour or vaseline and wrap a cloth about it wet with a solution of water and common baking soda.

If the clothing is afire, force the person to lie down immediately, wrap him in a blanket or other piece of cloth, preferably of woolen. Do not allow him to run around or expose himself to a draught. Fire may be extinguished by slapping the burning parts with a cloth, or throwing water upon the person, but the wrapping process is better, because it immediately smothers the fire, and water is not always available.

Slight scalds or burns may be relieved by the application of a solution made of a pint of water with one teaspoonful of baking soda or saleratus. Apply with a piece of lint, and then cover the burn or scald with absorbent cotton, held in place by a bandage. If the burn or scald is severe, apply sweet oil, olive oil, vaseline, or the white of an egg. If these are not handy, cover the spot with starch or use damp earth.

Burns caused by lye, and other alkaline chemicals, should be covered with water, then with vinegar, and then treated as those by fire.

Burns caused by acids and vitrol should be soaked with water and thoroughly washed with soda (saleratus) or lime water. Chalk or tooth powder may be used when saleratus is not available.

Carbolic acid burns may be treated with strong alcohol.

Burns of the mouth or throat coming from the drinking of hot fluids, may be treated by taking oil or the white of an egg into the mouth and allowing it to run into the throat if the throat is affected. Vinegar should be used for burns in the mouth coming from caustic potash and ammonia. If the burn is serious, summon the doctor.

Burns caused by gunpowder should be treated the same as are ordinary burns.

Shock or Collapse

Shock or collapse frequently occurs after serious accidents. It can be foretold generally, because the skin is cool and clammy, and it is usually accompanied with vomiting or rapid pulse, irregular breathing, or sighing, and the eyelids may be heavy, the pupils dilated, and the mind is not active. Insensibility frequently accompanies a shock. Send for a surgeon or doctor immediately. Place the patient in a warm bed, if possible, cover him with blankets, and allow his head to lie low. Remove all clothing, cutting it to save time. Wrap bandages around wounds or broken bones.

Hot cloths, or hot water bags, or a hot brick wrapped in cloth should be applied to the region of the heart, the pit of the stomach, and the feet. If wet cloths are used, wring them out frequently in hot water and re-apply them. It is not necessary to use heat sufficient to burn the skin. Under no circumstances apply heat to the head.

If possible, force the patient to drink hot water, hot tea, hot coffee, or hot milk. Malted milk is excellent, but it should be hot. Whisky and other alcoholic liquor should not be given, except by the advice of a doctor. Half a teaspoonful of aromatic spirits of ammonia in water may be given every 15 minutes for four doses, but not more. Stimulants should not be given after the patient begins to recover.

Vomiting may be stopped or relieved by administering a little brandy mixed with cracked ice.

If the skull is injured or there is concussion of the brain, with or without the appearance of apoplexy or severe breathing, do not administer a stimulant.

Sleeplessness.—Insomnia rapidly lowers the vital forces. It is due to several causes, including mental worry, indigestion, physical overexercise, and functional or organic diseases. Insomnia may be considered a natural warning of coming ailment. The cause should be located, and a good physician should be consulted. Sleep is encouraged by exercise in the open air and by taking hot drinks just before retiring. Hot malted milk is excellent; but solid food should not be taken just before retiring. Mild gymnastic exercise may be taken before an open window, but drugs should never be administered without the advice of a physician.

Snake Bite.—Do not waste valuable time to kill the snake. If the bite is venomous, rip open the clothing so that the wound will be exposed. Tie a handekrchief or rope around the arm or leg, above the bite. It should be drawn so tight that the circulation will be stopped or retarded. The use of a stick or pencil will assist in giving pressure. With a knife, open the holes made by the snake's fangs and cut around the wound liberally, being careful not to sever an artery. Let the blood run freely. Poison is sometimes removed by sucking a wound, but one should not do this if his lips are chapped or bleeding. The wound should be washed with soda solution and large doses of whisky or brandy should be administered. Call a surgeon immediately.

Sore Throat.—Sore throat may be merely local or be a forerunner of diphtheria. Better consult a physician.

Sprains.—Most sprains are serious, and a doctor should be called at once, but before he arrives the following simple treatment may be applied. Sprains twist and tear the ligaments and may rupture the small blood vessels. The flow of blood may be checked by application of cold or heat or by pressure. If the ankle or foot is sprained, wrap a folded towel tightly around the part sprained and then apply moist heat and elevate the leg. Immerse the foot in water as hot as can be borne and keep on adding hot water for about 20 minutes, so that the temperature may not be lowered; then apply a bandage, but continue the bathing treatment. Cold applications may be used instead of hot water, and should be applied by dipping cloths in ice water frequently, and wrapping them about the parts injured.

Stings of Poisonous Insects or of scorpions, centipedes, etc., should be treated with hartshorn, ammonia, after which cold water or cracked ice should be applied. Do not fail to call a surgeon or doctor. If the sting remains in the wound, remove it either by pressure on the skin or with a knife. The stings of common insects, such as mosquitoes, ants, etc., should be treated with a weak solution of ammonia, salt water, or a cloth wet with water in which a teaspoonful of baking soda to a pint of water is dissolved, may be bound on it.

Suffocation.—Always summon a physician. Place the patient in the air, remove all tight clothing about the neck and chest, and apply artificial respiration. Apply hot water in bottles to the body. Put mustard plasters above the heart, on the soles of his feet, and on his wrists. When the patient shows signs of recovering, give mild stimulants. If the patient is in a close room, open the windows and all of the doors. In rescue work do not open windows, but smash out all of the glass. In entering a room full of smoke, cover the mouth with a handkerchief wet with water or vinegar and water. Crawl on the floor, as the smoke is less dense near the floor. The rescuer should attach a rope to himself, so he can be pulled from his dangerous position.

Sunstroke.—Indications of sunstroke or heat prostration are a slow but full pulse, very labored breathing, and the skin is hot and dry, the face usually red, and the person affected is unconscious. Remove the sufferer to a shady place, and be sure to loosen his collar and clothing, if tight. Raise the head and shoulders. The head, face, and chest should be drenched with cold water, and if it is very hot use cracked ice. In ordinary cases of heat prostration, the patient is not unconscious, the skin is pale and clammy, and the breathing is not normal. Force the patient to lie on his back with his head level with his body, and loosen all tight clothing. Apply heat to the extremities, and cold to head. The patient should not be allowed to drink too much water. Give him hot drinks, and apply heat to the spine and feet. Under no circumstances administer alcoholic stimulants. Always send for a physician.

Temperature of the Body.—The normal body temperature is 98.4 degrees Fahrenheit. When it is higher, the patient is supposed to have a fever. Temperature usually rises in the afternoon, being one degree higher than in the first part of the night or in the early morning. It gradually falls from midnight to six or seven o'clock in the morning. The temperature of a child frequently rises two degrees from slight causes. Every family should carry a clinical thermometer. Bodily temperature should be taken by holding it in the mouth under the tongue for two minutes. Temperature under 101° indicates a slight fever; under 103° a moderate fever; under 105° a high fever. When the temperature rises two or three degrees above normal, send for a doctor at once.

Temperature of the Sick-Room.—Sixty-eight degrees Fahrenheit is a good average temperature for the sick-room. In certain diseases the average temperature may be lower, and for throat or chest affections it should be higher. When the patient is being washed or dressed, the temperature should be kept at about 70°.

Toothache.—If the nerve is exposed, or nearly so, toothache may be cured by placing in the cavity a small piece of cotton soaked in creosote or oil of cloves. If it continues, consult a dentist.

Transporting the Wounded.—Great care should be taken, because the slightest carelessness is likely to cause intense suffering. A four-handed seat may be made by two persons, the hands of each one clasping one of the wrists of the other, and two ordinary man can easily carry a person of average weight. A stretcher will carry the patient in a horizontal position if the persons carrying it place their hands under it. A stretcher may be made of boards, over which are placed coats or shawls, or a blanket may be fastened to two stout poles; if no poles are handy, a shawl tightly held by two persons will do, but great care should be taken to keep it tight. A window shutter is generally available. The sufferer should be very carefully placed upon the stretcher, and had better be lifted by several persons, by two at least. The bearers of the stretcher should not keep step, the opposite feet should be put forward at the same time to prevent the swaying of the stretcher and the rolling of the patient. Never carry the stretcher on the shoulders. Carry the patient feet foremost, except when going up hill. In case of a fractured thigh or leg, carry the patient head first when going down hill.

Ventilation.—The sick-room should never be without fresh air. Impure and close air breeds disease and encourages illness. Fresh air should be introduced constantly and steadily. The windows may be lowered at the top or patented ventilators used. To change the air, open the windows in an adjoining room, and then open the door between the rooms, but the fresh air in the adjoining room should be warm before it is allowed to penetrate the sick-room. By swinging the door back and forth, the air will be fanned in. Do not maintain the erroneous impression that cold air is pure because it is cold, for cold air may be as foul as warm air. Night air is not dangerous. The patient must breathe night air or closed-in day air, and closed-in air rapidly becomes foul.

Vomiting.—Lie down and hold small pieces of ice in your mouth. If it continues, consult a physician.

———o———

Wills.—A will, untechnically speaking, is virtually a bill-of-sale or transfer of property by its owner to those he may designate, but differs from the ordinary bill-of-sale in that there is no consideration mentioned on the part of those who will receive the property, and the will is not operative until the death of the maker of it. No one can execute a will unless he is presumably in his right mind, and knows what he is doing. Nor can a will be made by an idiot or one insane. The will must be signed and witnessed by several witnesses, each witness signing as a witness in the presence of all of the other witnesses. While it would appear that every one has a right to dispose of his property as he chooses, a will is not likely to stand in law if it can be proved that the maker of it was under undue or unfair influence, and, therefore, distributed his property to the prejudice of those who would be entitled to it if no will was made. For example: a will is not likely to hold good if its maker unfairly disowned close legal heirs, like a wife, husband, or children, or bequeathed his property to some institution which it could be shown he probably would not have done had not unfair pressure been brought to bear upon him at the time he made his will. All legal heirs should, as a rule, be mentioned in a will, even though they are given insignificant sums. As the laws differ in the several states, it is suggested that it is better and safer to consult a good lawyer, or one familiar with conditions.

Wireless Telegraphy.—The exact date of the discovery or invention of wireless telegraphy is not accurately known. Many scientists discovered it theoretically before Marconi made it practical. Some scientific authorities claim that it was originated by Professor Dolbear, of Massachusetts. Wireless telegraphy has been so perfected that it is now one of the ordinary means of communication throughout the world. Unscientifically speaking, wireless telegraphy consists of discharging powerful electrical currents into the atmosphere, their vibrations being taken up by the natural electricity in the air, and received by wires placed at an elevation. Practically all sea-going steamers are equipped with wireless telegraphy.

Woman's Suffrage.—The first convention in the interest of woman's rights was held July 19, 1908, at Seneca Falls, N. Y. In 1850, a National Woman's Rights Convention was held in Worcester, Mass. From that time woman's suffrage was agitated in America and in England, and many of the leading women of the world strongly advocated it. The World War gave a great impetus to woman suffrage, and in 1920 all the rights of franchise were granted to women of the United States. The States voting against woman suffrage were Alabama, Georgia, Mississippi, South Carolina, Virginia, Maryland, Delaware, Louisiana, and North Carolina. All other states ratified the amendment.

Women were granted the right to vote in New Zealand in 1893, in Australia in 1902, in Poland, England, Scotland, Ireland, Wales, Canada, Austria, Hungary, Czecho-Slovakia, and Germany, in 1918, and in Holland, Belgium, and Sweden in 1919.

Wool Industry.—The United States produces about $320,000,000 worth of wool in a year and weaves about 55,500,000 square yards, worth about $40,500,000.

World's Largest Steamships.—On page 204 is a list of the largest steamships plying the ocean (with former names of some of the vessels in parenthesis):

The following description of the "Berengaria" gives an idea of the immensity of a modern liner. The boat deck is 100 feet, and the trunks of the mast 246 feet, above the keel. The funnels are 69 feet long with oval openings, 29 by 18 feet. The rudder alone weighs 90 tons. She is registered at 50,000 tons, with

Name.	Regist'd Tonnage.	Length, Feet.	Breadth Feet.
Majestic (Bismarck)	56,000	956	100
Leviathan (Vaterland)	54,282	950	100
Berengaria (Imperator)	52,000	898	97
Olympic	46,439	883	92
Aquitania	45,647	901	92
Homeric (Columbus)	35,000	775	76
Paris	33,700	768	86
Mauretania	32,000	790	83
George Washington	25,570	722	78
Empress of Scotland (Kaiserin Auguste Victoria)	24,581	677	77
Belgenland (Belgic)	24,547	671	78
Adriatic	24,541	726	75
Rotterdam	24,170	668	77
Baltic	23,876	726	75
France	23,666	720	75
America (Amerika)	22,622	687	74
Duilio	22,000	662	80
Cedric	21,040	680	75
Scythia	21,000	600	73
Celtic	20,904	680	75
Minnesota	20,602	622	73
Cappolonio	20,597	638	72
Wm. Oswald	20,000	588	72

a displacement of 70,000 tons. Displacement represents the weight of the water which is occupied by that part of the hull under water. The ship is a modern floating hotel, containing a grill-room, a tea garden, a veranda café, several ladies' sitting-rooms, a palm garden, a ball room, a gymnasium, a swimming tank, and other accessories. In the first cabin there are 220 regular bath rooms and showers, including 150 private bath rooms. The state-rooms do not contain berths, metal bedsteads being used throughout. The entrance hall is 90 feet wide, and 69 feet long. In addition the vessel carries a drug store, a book store, and a flower shop, and several passenger elevators are maintained. To illuminate the ship there are 9,500 electric lamps. The Roman bath is 65 feet long, and 41 feet wide. The swimming bath is 39 feet long, 21 feet wide, and 9 feet deep. The quadruple turbine engines have 72,000 horse-power and develop an average speed of 22½ knots an hour. One of the immense rotars contains 50,000 blades, and weighs 135 tons. The ship carries a crew of 1,100 persons, a complete fire department, and wireless telegraphy. If the "Berengaria" was set on end, she would be higher than the largest building in the world, which is 750 feet high. The ship has a passenger capacity equal to the population of a large town.

Yankee.—This word is said to be a corruption of English or Anglais, pronounced by the Massachusetts Indians, who gave this name to the New England Colonists, Yenghies, Yanghies, Yankees. It was applied to the New Englanders by the British soldiers during the Revolutionary War, and to the Federal soldiers by the Confederates during the Civil War.

Yankee Doodle.—The origin of Yankee Doodle, perhaps the most famous American national air, is unknown. It is supposed to have been an English tune. At any rate, it was introduced into America by the British troops in 1775.

INDEX

INDEX

i

INDEX

INDEX

INDEX

iv

INDEX

v

INDEX

INDEX

vii

INDEX

INDEX

INDEX

INDEX

INDEX

INDEX

COSIMO CLASSICS

COSIMO is an innovative publisher of books that inspire, inform, and engage readers worldwide.

COSIMO was inspired by Cosimo de Medici, the first of the de Medici dynasty, who ignited the most important cultural and artistic revolution in Western history — the Renaissance.

Cosimo de Medici, the quintessential Renaissance man, was a banker, political leader, scholar, and patron of the arts. He had a passion for the pursuit of knowledge, and he breathed new life into the study of the ancient past. He enriched Florence by building palaces and churches and by sponsoring libraries, where professional scribes copied classics from antiquity into the finest manuscripts.

This quest for enrichment is the foundation for **COSIMO,** an innovative publisher of books that inspire, inform, and engage readers worldwide. **COSIMO CLASSICS** brings to life unique, out-of-print classics, representing subjects as diverse as *Alternative Health, Business and Economics, Eastern Philosophy, Personal Growth, Mythology, Philosophy, Sacred Texts, Science, Spirituality,* and much more!

COSIMO CLASSICS uses state-of-the art technology to publish distinctive, high-quality books that are always available online at affordable prices.

COSIMO CLASSICS

COSIMO CLASSICS uses state-of-the-art technology to publish distinctive, high-quality books. In our pursuit for enrichment, our commitment to you is that **COSIMO CLASSICS** offers:

> ➢ **Permanent Availability:** Our books never go out of print.

> ➢ **Global Availability**: Our books are available online at www.cosimobooks.com, www.amazon.com, www.barnesandnoble.com, and other online bookstores, and can be ordered from your favorite local bookstore, too.

> ➢ **Special Quantity Discounts:** Our books are available at special quantity discounts for bulk purchases, sales promotions, premiums, or fund raising. For more information, please contact us at info@cosimobooks.com.

> ➢ **Free e-Newsletter:** Sign up for our e-newsletter at www.cosimobooks.com to discover what's happening at **COSIMO** and to receive announcements of our new books, free excerpts, and special offers.

Your Favorite Out-of-Print Books: If you know of any books that you would like to see republished as a **COSIMO CLASSIC**, drop us a line at info@cosimobooks.com.

A complete collection of **COSIMO CLASSICS** is always available at our website, www.cosimobooks.com.

Made in the USA
Las Vegas, NV
02 December 2021

35868347R00135